Benjamin Franklin Award Finalist - Best Book

Get Into Any College

Secrets Of Harvard Students

- ■ Step-By-Step Instructions On How To Get Into & Pay For Any College
- ■ Learn From The True-Life Successes & Grave Failures Of Actual Students
- ■ The Only Book On College Admissions That Combines Entertainment, Fun, & Education
- ■ Comprehensive—The Only Resource You Will Ever Need On Admissions & Financial Aid

JIM GOOD & LISA LEE

Check out our website at: www.supercollege.com

Get Into Any College: Secrets Of Harvard Students
By Jim Good and Lisa Lee

Published by 101 Publishing
4546 B10 El Camino Real, Suite 281
Los Altos, California 94022

Photo courtesy of Candace Chan Yee. Edited by Bob Drews.

ISBN 0-9657556-3-0

Manufactured in the United States of America
10 9 8 7 6 5 4 3 2

Cataloging-in-Publication Data
Jim Good, Lisa Lee
     Get Into Any College: Secrets Of Harvard Students / by Jim Good and Lisa Lee. —1st ed.
               p.   cm.
     Includes appendices and index.
     ISBN 0-9657556-3-0
     1. College Admissions I. Title
     2. Education 3. Reference

Contents At-A-Glance

• • • • • • • • • • • • •

www.supercollege.com

Special Highlights

• • • • • • • • • • •

Stories From Real Life

• • • • • • • • • • • • • •

These short stories about the successes and failures of real students are both entertaining and enlightening. They reveal how the college admissions and financial aid process really works!

Contents

• • • • • •

Master the verbal and reading tests • How to be a math whiz • The day before the big event • Test time tips • A timeline for testing • Three's a crowd • How to deal with a bombed test

To our families.

To Harvard and Stanford.

To the many students and friends who shared their college admissions experiences, secrets, successes, and failures.

Also, to all those who will soon embark upon the most exciting journey of their lives—college.

DISCOVER THE KEY TO
THE IVY GATES

In This Chapter

▲ A Preview Of How This Book Will Help You Get In

▲ Our Revolutionary Approach & A Peek At What's Inside

▲ Stories From Real Life: You Can Be Normal & Still Get Into Harvard

▲ Who We Are & Why You Should Listen To Us

▲ Steps To Success: A College Admissions Time Line

How This Book Will Help You Get Into Your Dream School

If you ever visit Harvard you will find nestled among the red brick buildings in the heart of Harvard Yard a statue of John Harvard. Like a miniature Lincoln memorial, old John is seated in a chair upon a pedestal, dressed in the latest 18th century fashion and clutching a large encyclopedic book. John has greeted millions of students and visitors alike and has the reputation of being America's third most photographed statue. (He has also had the dubious honor of being painted blue by those rascal Yalies during the Harvard-Yale football game.) There are three things about this distinguished statue, however, that are commonly referred to as the "three lies" of Harvard. They are:

#1 The date inscribed for Harvard's founding is incorrect.

#2 The statue is not of John Harvard but of a better looking stand-in.

#3 Harvard was not founded by John Harvard (although he did give a lot of money).

Along with these "three lies" we would like to add another:

#4 You have to be a superstar to get into Harvard.

The truth about selective colleges (which include much more than the Harvards, Yales, and Stanfords of this country) is that the majority of high school students who apply have the skills and talents required to succeed at these schools. However, within this large group of qualified students only those few who can successfully convey their abilities, talents, and personalities in the short space of the college application will have any chance of getting accepted. The 12% of applicants who got into Harvard last year, for example, were not the only ones capable of doing Harvard quality work. Rather these 12% were best able to write that special kind of application that convinced the admissions officers to select them to fill the limited spaces in the freshman class.

We have written this book with only one goal: to help you create that kind of winning application. Written entirely by a group of Ivy League graduates, we feel that this book is the best no-nonsense, hands-on, how-to manual for any high school student who wants to get into any college.

If you have decent grades, don't bomb the SAT or ACT, are a reasonably hard worker, and (most important) are willing to challenge yourself academically, then you probably have what it takes to get into a selective school. But, with many thousands of other applicants who are equally qualified you need to write an application that not only maximizes your strengths (while minimizing your weaknesses) but also insures that you stand out from among the masses. Can writing this type of application be learned? Certainly! And we, who have done so, will teach you how.

Traditional books on admissions often take a top-down approach filled with useless lectures by supposed "experts," many of whose firsthand experiences are decades old. This book is built on the actual tips, strategies, and secrets discovered by today's students who have gotten into top private and state universities. Based on these up-to-date techniques, you will learn how to create that winning application that will help get you into any school.

So let us be your guide through the college admissions process. We will show you what works and (almost as important) what doesn't. By the time you finish this book you will have produced the best possible college application and, with a little luck, (you always need luck in this game!) you will receive in the spring that beautifully thick envelope with an acceptance letter from the school of your dreams.

Why This Book Is Superior To All Others: A Shameless (But True) Testimonial

We know that you have many choices when it comes to buying a book on college admissions. If you are standing in the bookstore reading this, we hope the following will highlight some of the distinguishing merits of this book that we feel make it the best and only resource on college admissions and financial aid you will ever need. (If you have already bought this book then you may skip this section, or read it if you want to see just how smart a purchase you've made!)

1 A Down-To-Earth Radically Different Approach From Any Other Guide. Unlike other books written by so-called "experts," this book was written by those who have actually done it. With the help of dozens of students from both elite private and highly selective public colleges, we share with you the secrets of how to get in. All of the strategies and tips in this book have been proven successful by students much like yourself. Plus, you will learn about some common mistakes that can turn an otherwise strong application into a guaranteed rejection.

2 Absolutely Essential Examples, Samples, And Illustrations. Any how-to book worth the paper it is printed on should provide many examples so you can see how the tips and strategies are actually used. Not only have we included examples from real applications in every chapter, but we have even included 23 real examples of college essays.

3 No Wasted Time With Fluff Or Padding. Unlike other tomes that are often filled with fluff and time wasting ruminations, this guide gives you all the right information—comprehensively and concisely. You will not find much about evaluating your strengths, why you should go to college, or how to choose a college. (We trust you can decide for yourself whether Harvard or Yale is more to your liking.) What you will learn are the much more important strategies on how to get in. Plus, no high school student has the time (or desire) to read a marginally helpful 350 page book about colleges and admissions.

❹ Stories From Real Life: The Successes And Failures Of Actual Students. There is no better way to understand the seemingly mysterious process of college admissions than through the experiences of those who have already done it. Learn from the grand successes and grave mistakes of actual students through their uncensored and honest confessions. Each short story not only reveals how the admissions process really works but is also quite entertaining. (We promise at least a few laughs—not an inconsequential point considering the work ahead of you!)

❺ This Book Is Just Plain Ol' Fun To Read. Although the college admissions process has historically been the diametric opposite of the word "fun," we feel that if you're going to spend your valuable time reading this book then the least we can do is make it entertaining. That's why throughout the book you'll find many personal stories and anecdotes that, aside from teaching you more about college admissions, are also pretty funny.

What's Inside: A Sneak Preview

Now that we have shamelessly praised our book, let's take a quick look at what's inside. In general, each chapter gives step-by-step, easy-to-follow instructions on how to complete a particular part of the application process. Along with essential Do's and Don'ts you will also learn about common pitfalls—many of which were painfully discovered by the students in this book.

Being the perceptive authors that we are, we have designed the chapters to be read in sequence or independently, depending on your personal needs. So, feel free to skip to the chapters that you think you need help on the most.

Chapter 1: Discover The Key To The Ivy Gates. What you are reading right now.

Chapter 2: The Neapolitan Approach To Picking Schools. We don't want to waste your time with too much talk about to which schools you should apply. But, it has come to our attention that given the expense of college applications (most schools charge at least $50 a pop), it will be useful to lay out our unique strategy to insure that you maximize your chances for getting into the best college without spending too much time or money.

Chapter 3: Create A Stunning Application Form. Here we will take you on a guided tour of the blanks, spaces, and boxes of the application form and show you how to fill them out correctly. There are many Do's and Don'ts for the application form and by learning what information to list and what to withhold, you can create an application that will stand out from the pile.

Chapter 4: How To Get The Right Evaluations. There is plenty that you can do (none of it unethical, of course) to insure that your teachers write glowing evaluations. This chapter answers the two most important questions: Who are the best people to ask for evaluations? And how can you be sure that they will write unique and positive reviews?

Chapter 5: How To Write An Irresistible Essay. How can you possibly write about the past 17-odd years of your life in fewer words than are on the back of a cereal box? We'll show you how in this essay-writing workshop. Here you will master the secrets to writing a compelling personal essay that will have admissions officers lining up to offer you admission. The essay is by far the most important part of the application, and if you only have time to read one chapter, this should be it.

Chapter 6: The Magic Of Recycling Essays. This single chapter will save you weeks if not months of time. Recycling is the all important, some would claim magical, technique that allows you to use only a few quality essays for all college and scholarship applications. Following the simple and creative editing strategies in this chapter you can apply to as many schools as you want using only a handful of original essays.

Chapter 7: Example Essays: The Good, Bad, & Ugly. This chapter contains—you guessed it—the example essays. Included are 14 essays that worked as well as 7 that didn't. A short commentary follows each essay written from the perspective of an admissions officer. You can use the good essays as models to compare to your own. The bad ones, of course, show you how *not* to write an essay.

Chapter 8: The Secrets Of The Interview. Are you worried about going one on one with an admissions officer or alumnus? Well don't be. After reading this chapter you will understand why. You will also get a sneak peek at the kinds of questions your interviewers will ask, learn how to present yourself as the intelligent and motivated applicant that you are, and find the solution to the all important issue of what to wear.

Chapter 9: Put On Those Finishing Touches. Whew! You have worked hard and now have a set of outstanding applications. But before you mail those thick packets to the colleges there are some important things you need to double check. Here you will find a fascinating discussion about your various postal options as well as what to do if (oh, my goodness) you miss the deadline!

Chapter 10: The Alphabet Soup Of Tests: How To Ace Them. Standardized tests are one of the most dreaded parts of college admissions. Here we discuss how important these tests *really* are and give you over 50 hints on how to increase your scores. This chapter has everything you ever wanted to know about the SAT I, ACT, SAT II, PSAT, TOEFL, and AP exams.

Chapter 11: How To Win Free Cash For College. If you thought getting in was difficult, consider for a moment how you (and your parents) are going to foot the bill. Fortunately, there is more money out there to help you pay for school than you may think. Financing your education can come not only through college and government funding and outside scholarships but also by bargaining, in the right way, with the university to increase its share of the cost. This chapter is devoted entirely to the many ways to finance your education—a topic particularly popular among parents.

Chapter 12: Get Started Before Your Senior Year: For Freshmen, Sophomores, And Juniors. If you are not a senior but know that you want to attend a competitive school, then it is very important for you to get a head start. To help, we have designed this chapter especially for you on how to plan your remaining years in high school to maximize your chances of getting into a good college. Included are keys to picking impressive classes, getting your teachers to love you, and choosing how and to what degree to get involved with the often overlooked but very important extracurricular activities and sports.

You Can Be Normal And Still Get Into Harvard

I am living proof that you don't have to be a superstar to get into Harvard. Although I went to a competitive high school, I was far from being an outstanding student. Unlike my friends who had perfect 4.0s, my report card was littered with "B's." I did get "A's," but still my transcript was nothing to get excited about. I got average SAT scores. They weren't terrible, but they weren't great either. I was a member of a few groups although my highest position was secretary for my school's public service club. I have to admit that when I filled out my college applications even I was shocked at how "average" I was on paper.

My only chance I felt was to work really hard on the essay and hopefully get good teacher evaluations. I don't know what my teachers wrote, but it must not have been that bad. I was the kind of student who always tried hard. I also spent a lot of time on my essay and must have written and rewritten it a dozen or more times. But still nobody ever imagined that I would get into Harvard.

Was everyone shocked when April came. Even I was stunned when I opened the acceptance letter. In fact, soon after I arrived at Harvard my roommates and I had a late night discussion about how we got in. We began to compare SATs, grades, and anything else to see why we were chosen. When I told them what I had gotten they couldn't help but tease, "How in the world did you get in?"

It was pretty obvious that it was not my grades, scores or activities that got me in. I think I owe it mostly to my essay and evaluations. My point is not that admissions is arbitrary (I think the opposite is true), but I hope all of you who are thinking about applying to Harvard will not be discouraged just because others have better grades, higher scores, or are more active in clubs or sports. As I found out, it's not a prerequisite for you to be School President, valedictorian, and football team captain all at the same time to get into Harvard.

Harvard does take normal people too. At first I was embarrassed at how low my scores and grades were in comparison to my roommates. But now I freely admit my "averageness." And Harvard must know a little something about success since I have consistently gotten better grades than my roommates who, based on their high school records, are far more outstanding than I.

By: Eugene S. who is at Harvard and is still normal.

Chapter 13: Groom Your Child Into Harvard: A Parents' Guide To Helping Without Hurting. Many parents want to help their child get into college but don't necessarily know what to do (besides pulling out the checkbook). In fact, some forms of parental involvement can be detrimental to getting a child admitted. If you are a parent, then you will find this chapter (along with the rest of the book) especially enlightening. You will learn everything you need to know about helping junior or juniorette get into an elite school as well as how to pay for this education without having to take out a second mortgage.

Chapter 14: Decide Which Ivy Gate To Enter. Here we skip to spring when you will be hearing from all of the colleges. We give you some advice on how to decide which offer to accept as well as how to deal with (the words every student dreads), the Wait List.

The Admissions Gamble And The Importance Of Luck

In all of our experience helping students get in, one very clear fact about college admissions has become apparent: There are no guarantees. Many well-qualified and deserving applicants are denied. The exact criteria that admissions committees employ on the individual level are just too diverse to predict. And there is clearly an element of luck and circumstance that can help or hurt a student's chances. This can be viewed both positively and negatively. On the one hand, just because you didn't get a perfect SAT score doesn't mean you won't get into Harvard. On the other hand, even if you are well qualified and you do everything right, you can for reasons entirely beyond your control still be denied.

The information in this book is designed to help you write the best possible application, which is essential to gain admission to the most competitive schools. We do not, however, guarantee in any way admittance into any school. No one can make such a guarantee, and if you meet someone who does, he or she is lying.

Who We Are And Why You Should Listen To Us

You may be wondering who we are and what special credentials we have to write a book about college admissions. Well, since you've twisted our arms–ouch!–we suppose we will have to do a little bragging–which, by the way, is an important "art" you will have to learn to write a successful application.

Between the two of us we applied to and were accepted by all of the Ivy League schools plus Stanford, Berkeley, Duke, Rice, Pomona, and a host of other prestigious state and private institutions. We are also some of the few Harvard graduates who can say that we were not rejected by any college or university. Both of us recently graduated Magna Cum Laude. Jim is currently pursuing his Ph.D. at Stanford and Lisa is working in marketing for a large newspaper.

We should also mention that we are not the only "authors" since this book draws on the collective experiences of many other Ivy League students too numerous to name individually but who generously shared their time to be interviewed, shamelessly contributed their personal stories (both good and bad), and allowed us to print their application essays. Without the gracious cooperation of these students and friends, this book would not have been possible.

Steps to Success:
Your Timeline For
College Admissions

9th Grade

• • • • • • • • • • • • • • • • • •

Fall Semester

Get acquainted with your teachers, the coursework, and the activities offered at your school.

Spring Semester

Make a preliminary plan for the courses you will take in high school. Include challenging AP or Honors courses.

Meet your counselor and ask what resources your school has for learning more about colleges.

Explore extracurricular activities.

Summer Vacation

Find a summer job, do volunteer work, or attend a summer program.

If you go on a family vacation, be sure to visit colleges in the area.

10th Grade

• • • • • • • • • • • • • • • •

September - November

Take challenging courses including AP or Honors classes. Keep up your grades—aim for "A's."

Compete in matches, contests, and competitions to rack up some awards and honors.

Start to dedicate yourself to a few extracurricular activities, and work toward a leadership position. Also, consider starting a club or publishing something in the school newspaper or literary magazine.

Think about taking the PSAT in October. Check with your counselor.

December - February

Get in touch with alums from your school who are back from college for vacation. Go to college fairs, and glance through college guidebooks.

Meet with your counselor to discuss what you should be doing to prepare for applying to college.

March - May

Take the AP tests in May in subjects that you have completed.

If you feel prepared enough, take SAT II exams (usually in May or June) in subjects that you have completed.

Summer Vacation

Find a summer job, do volunteer work, or attend a summer program.

If you go on a family vacation, again visit colleges in the area.

Start preparing for the PSAT.

11th Grade

• • • • • • • • • • • • • • • •

September - November

Take the PSAT in October to practice for the SAT I and be eligible for National Merit Scholarship awards.

Continue to take challenging AP or Honors courses and maintain good grades.

Get to know your favorite teachers well. Start thinking about who you might ask to write evaluations.

Focus on becoming a leader in a few extracurricular activities—run for an office, lead a team, or start your own club, business, or service project.

Get a copy of some college applications to preview.

Continue to compete in matches, contests, and competitions.

December - February

Discuss with your parents how you will finance your education. Ask your counselor about any local or regional scholarships.

Continue to research colleges by talking to alumni, going to college fairs, and reading college directories and brochures.

Register and prepare for the SAT I or ACT and SAT II exams. Think about review classes or set up your own preparation schedule.

March - May

Take the SAT I (usually in March or May) or the ACT (usually in April).

Take AP exams in May and the SAT II exams in June.

Visit your college advisor or counselor to discuss your preliminary plans for applying to college and sources of financial aid.

Write to your U.S. Senator or Representative if you would like to attend a U.S. military academy or participate in an ROTC program.

Summer

Find a summer job, do volunteer work, or attend a summer program.

Plan family vacations so that you can also visit some of the colleges where you might want to apply.

Write to colleges for applications.

Register and prepare for the SAT I or ACT and SAT II. Set up a schedule to study for these exams or take a test prep class.

Research and begin applying to outside scholarships.

12th Grade
● ● ● ● ● ● ● ● ● ● ● ● ● ● ● ● ●

September - November

Continue to take challenging courses and keep up your grades—aim for "A's." Be careful of the "senior slump."

Make sure you have all of the college applications. Decide which schools you will apply to using the *Neapolitan Approach*. (See Chapter 2.)

Make a list of each college's deadlines!

Research and apply to outside scholarships. Check your local library for reference books which list various scholarships.

Take the SAT I (usually in October or November) or the ACT (usually in October).

Take the SAT II exams in November or December.

If you are applying for *Early Action,* finish taking the necessary standardized tests. The November tests are typically the last that you can take to be eligible for *Early Action.*

Submit your *Early Action* application. Deadlines are typically around November 1, but check with individual schools as some may be earlier.

Ask teachers and counselors to complete your Evaluation Forms and School Report. Make sure you approach them early and make clear the deadlines for each school.

Brainstorm for and write your essays, and enlist editors to help you perfect them. (Be sure to start this as early as possible!)

Arrange college interviews and practice for them.

December - February

Send off your applications—Deadlines are typically January 1, but check with each school.

Complete the necessary financial aid forms, including the FAFSA and PROFILE. Both are typically due February 1 to be eligible for financial aid from the college.

Continue to apply to outside scholarships. Don't forget to check with local civic groups and with your parents' employers.

Ask your counselor to complete any necessary Mid-Year School Reports. They are typically due in February.

March - May

You are done (almost)! Now it's time to wait it out. You will typically receive notification letters at the beginning of April. (Remember good news usually but not always comes in thick envelopes.)

Decision time: with help from your parents, teachers, and counselor decide where you'd like to spend the next four years. Discuss with your parents the financial aid offers and contact the schools if they are seriously insufficient. Take part in "Pre-Frosh" events and visitations. Notify the schools of your decision and send in your deposit to your new college.

If you haven't already, send thank you letters to all of your helpers, and inform them of where you have decided to attend.

Summer

Enjoy your summer of freedom. Congratulations and good luck as you embark on four of the most exciting years of your life!

THE NEAPOLITAN APPROACH TO PICKING SCHOOLS

In This Chapter
- ▲ The "Right" Number Of Schools To Apply To
- ▲ Hedge Your Bets: Spread Your Choices Intelligently
- ▲ Essential Questions To Ask About Each College
- ▲ Legacies, Minorities, Jocks, & Foreign Students

The Overstated Problem Of Where To Apply

Many thousands of trees have been sacrificed to produce the paper on which countless authors have written about deciding where to apply. Although picking where to apply is an important decision, it depends a lot on personal preferences. (One student we know of picked schools based on the quality of the paper used for their informational letters.) Since preferences vary, we will not be so presumptuous as to assume we know what is important to you. What we will do in this chapter, however, is present the factors which we feel you will want to keep in mind when deciding where to apply.

One question which always seems to worry high school seniors is to how many schools they should apply. While there is always the occasional student who applies to more than 20 schools—we know of one student who applied to 37—we feel that this is definitely overkill. Most students apply to between six and nine schools. This is a reasonable number, especially considering the fact that each school will charge between $35 to $60 just for the privilege of applying. Plus, by "recycling" your essays (more on this in Chapter 6) or using the Common Application, applying to this number of schools should be easy.

So without wasting any more trees, let's look at how to decide where to apply.

Hedge Your Bets: The Neapolitan Ice Cream Approach

Think of colleges as Neapolitan ice cream. (Just bear with us a moment and the value of thinking of colleges as that tri-flavor ice cream will become clear.) For our families, the strawberry ice cream was always the least desirable and the last flavor remaining in the box, the vanilla was likable and delicious, but the chocolate was the flavor which everyone fought over. While your order of preference may be different, like Neapolitan ice cream, colleges may also be divided into three different categories of desirability.

The Colleges As Neapolitan Ice Cream

Strawberry: These are schools to which you are almost definitely sure that you will be accepted, schools where you know that your grade point average is well above the median, and schools that have a reputation for having less strenuous requirements for admission.

Vanilla: These are the schools where you are pretty sure you will be accepted and that you would like, but perhaps not love, to attend. They are the schools that fulfill most of your preferences.

Chocolate: These are your top-choice schools for which you would give up all your earthly possessions to attend. Most likely these are the schools to which it is the most difficult to gain admission. Even if you think that you don't have a chance, apply anyway. The admissions officers might find you to be a more remarkable person than you believe you are. (It has been our experience that some of the most extraordinary people at Harvard have also been the most modest.)

Most students pick a few colleges as their strawberry flavor. The majority of schools are usually of the vanilla variety. And depending on how competitive they believe their applications are, they may have a few or many chocolate schools. Regardless of how your list turns out, just make sure that you have schools of each flavor and that they are schools that generally meet your preferences.

The schools that you are sure you can get into but that you don't have a strong desire to attend are the strawberry flavor. The schools that are selective but which you still have a good shot at and wouldn't mind attending are the vanilla ice cream. And the highly selective schools (Harvard accepts only around 12% of those who apply) are the chocolate. When deciding where to apply make sure that you have a couple of schools in each flavor.

The Neapolitan Ice Cream Approach insures that you will definitely have a place to go without selling yourself short by not trying for the top schools.

Which School Has The Best Parties And Other Less Serious Questions You Need To Ask

One student used the *U.S. News & World Report* annual college rankings as her only criteria for applying to college, thinking that these rankings were the best and only way to select good colleges. She was accepted by three of the five top colleges to which she applied. Only one problem: she realized later that she didn't want to relocate to the East Coast! This is a good illustration that although you can choose schools by name and reputation, it is better to have concrete reasons for applying.

Once you know generally what you want from a college you will need to do some research on those intangibles that will make your college years rewarding academically, socially, and culturally. One of the first places to look is in those beautiful full-color brochures that came along with the applications. These brochures are filled with lots of useful information, but remember, they do tend to be a little biased. In addition, you should also consult one of the many guides to colleges. Here you can find general information as well as some useful statistics—such as how many freshmen are admitted each year.

However, don't just settle for pictures and printed words. Go to college fairs and speak with the college representatives. For a schedule of national fairs, write to the National Association of College Admissions Counselors. See Appendix A for the address. Also speak to recent graduates of your high school who are now attending the schools. If the school is close to you, visit the campus, take a tour, and ask to be put in touch with a current student to ask him or her some questions.

Most schools now have home pages on the World Wide Web, and you may want to click around them to learn more. In Appendix B we have listed some useful Internet addresses.

While perusing the various information about the schools, keep the following questions in mind:

What Are Your Academic Goals?

▶ Do you want to be trained for a specific line of work or do you want a general education? A pre-professional education prepares you for a specific job or position and includes areas such as engineering and pre-med. Some schools like MIT have very strong programs for those interested in the sciences, but might not be right for someone interested in comparative literature. A liberal arts education, on the other hand, does not limit you to training for a specific job but equips you with knowledge and reasoning skills suitable for many jobs.

▶ What might you major in? Most universities have departments that excel in certain areas but are only average in others. While it may be too early for you to know whether you want to major in English or History, you should check out how strong the programs are in the fields you are considering.

▶ Do you prefer a small college or large university setting? Most students find smaller classes that allow more active participation more rewarding than large, impersonal lectures. But larger institutions also have advantages, such as more resources and often (but not always) more famous faculty.

▶ How many years does it take to graduate? Most schools graduate their students in four years, but some majors may take longer.

Do You Want To Attend Party Central?

▶ Do you want to have three Greek letters emblazoned on your chest everywhere you go? Does the school have a Greek system?

Some students are very much inclined to joining a fraternity or sorority, while others feel that their existence on campus is over-bearing for those who choose not to go Greek.

▶ Does the school offer extracurricular activities that you would enjoy? For example, if you join the Hasty Pudding Club at Harvard you'll have the chance to cross-dress and sing on stage at its famous annual performance.

What Type Of Digs Do You Want?

▶ Do most students live on campus or commute? Whether students spend most of their lives on campus or off makes a big difference in the social atmosphere of the college.

▶ Can you live with strangers? Can you bathe near strangers? If you lived in the dorm, would you have roommates? How modern or ancient are the dorms?

What Kind Of Campus Environment Do You Want?

▶ What size student body fits you? Some students like intimate schools where they know the names of all of their classmates, while others prefer the advantages of belonging to a large student body.

▶ Is the campus in the inner city, countryside, or somewhere in between? Is it a college town where the college is the center of the city? Is it in the middle of nowhere, where you have to drive 40 miles just to see a movie?

▶ What is the weather like? If you've never endured a minus-20 degree winter or a 90 percent humidity summer, you might want to think twice about how the weather will affect your life (e.g., being able to sunbathe between classes vs. literally not seeing the sun for months at a time).

▶ How far is the college from home? Do you want to remain geographically close to your family and friends, or do you want to venture into the world of collegedom solo, farther from home?

▶ Is the school known for attracting students of a particular political view? Most schools have a surprisingly even balance of conservative and liberal students. However a few have an imbalance towards one over the other. While you should keep this in mind, don't let this be an overriding factor since you will almost always find others who share (and oppose) your views.

These questions are just guidelines. You may not be able to find answers to all of them, but certainly consider them when applying. After you narrow down your list, start to classify the schools by their flavor according to the Neapolitan Approach. Make sure that you have a few schools of each type on your list.

Special Treatment For Special Groups

When checking out which colleges to apply to, you need to check out yourself, too. You may have a special quality that will increase your chance of getting admitted. These special qualities include being a legacy, a minority, an athlete, or an international student. Most colleges treat these groups of students specially, and this might affect where you choose to apply and possibly where you are admitted.

So There's A Building On Campus Named After You

When we were at Harvard there was a young woman who shared the same last name as one of the dorms in Harvard Yard. We don't doubt her qualifications for being admitted to the college, but we are sure that it certainly didn't hurt her chances that her grandparents had donated enough money to have the building named after them.

Legacies are students who are children of alumni, namely alumni who donate money to the college. When you apply, you may hear that some colleges give preference to the children of former graduates. Admissions officers often explain that this is because the college wants to build an established alumni community based on family relationships. This sounds nice, but the true reason for giving preference to legacies is that admitting them also results in an increase in the donations to the college by its alumni. After all, if you were a Harvard alumnus whose child also got accepted to your alma mater you, too, might feel grateful enough to contribute just a little more money, right?

Although we may think that applicants should be treated equally regardless of their family's educational history or financial situation, the truth of the matter is that those students whose parents and grandparents attended the same university and whose parents have wings of buildings named after them because of their large donations have an advantage. Thus, you will probably want to apply to your parents' alma mater, especially if they have made financial contributions to the college's fundraisers. Of course, just because your parents went to a certain college does not mean you will automatically be accepted. You will still need to present a strong application.

Minority Groups

This is something that of course is out of your control, but some colleges do give preference to students who are members of underrepresented minority groups. Colleges want to create diverse student bodies with representation that more or less reflects the general population. African-Americans, Hispanic-Americans, and Native-Americans are usually viewed as underrepresented groups. Asian-Americans are less and less being considered a minority, although some ethnic groups do still qualify.

Recently, some schools have been moving away from using such preferences, and there is no way to determine how much greater your chances are for being accepted based on whether or not a school gives preferences for certain minority groups. Our advice is to not consider what the specific policy of the school is. You will never be admitted to a school based on your ethnic background alone.

Score As A Jock

Chances are that if you regularly score 80 points in the state championship basketball tournaments, you will have no trouble finding places to apply since many colleges (or at least those strong in basketball) will seek you. Most schools have a whole entourage of coaches and athletic directors who are paid large salaries to find athletes to fill their teams.

If you are recruited by colleges for your athletic ability, kudos to you. Double kudos if you are offered a scholarship as well. Our only advice is that you think not only about which school has the strongest team or is offering the sweetest deal but that you consider the academic standards as well. If you aren't professional team material, then you will certainly need to put your college degree into action after you retire your team jersey.

Coming To America: International Students

With thousands of schools from which to select, the U.S. is certainly a great place to get an education as an international student. Just as with an American student, however, you need to figure out which are the best schools to which you should apply. The questions in this chapter will certainly help you decide. But, you should consider these factors as well:

Does the school provide financial aid for international students? Does the school have special programs, clubs, counseling, or housing for international students? What are the English ability requirements? (You will probably have to score a certain minimum on the TOEFL exam.) Are there courses in English as a Second Language (ESL) offered during the term or in the summer before your first year? Will you be able to live in campus housing? (This is especially important for your first year since finding an apartment while adjusting to a new environment is very difficult and time consuming.) Finally, make sure you will be able to obtain the correct visa to live, study, and possibly work in the U.S.

The Sky's The Limit So Don't Worry About Money (Yet)

Until now, we have not discussed perhaps the biggest factor in determining where you will go to college—money. Yes, it is true that college costs a bundle, with private colleges being especially guilty of high prices. It is not uncommon for parents to take out a second mortgage on their homes or for students to be burdened with loans for years after they graduate. And unfortunately, the costs are only rising.

However, at this point, do not worry about money. Even if money is tight, don't make it your primary concern just yet. If you will have trouble paying for the application fee, ask your counselor about a fee waiver.

Why I Wish I Had Chosen Better

When I was a senior in high school I had no idea where I wanted to go to college. I remembered someone saying good things about "California College." (This is a fictitious name since I do not want to offend this very real school.)

One day I received an information packet from California College. Inside was a beautiful full-color brochure which unfolded into this gorgeous picture of the school. Along with the pictures were dozens of testimonials by students and faculty praising the small student-to-teacher ratio and wonderful extracurricular activities. After reading all these good things and seeing the fantastic pictures, I felt that I just had to apply to this school. I quickly returned the reply card and a few weeks later received an application.

I spent several weeks filling out the application. When I received my acceptance letters, I only had to look at the happy students in the California College brochure to make up my mind. I wanted to be one of those smiling students. On August 25th my parents and I arrived at LAX. We rented a car and headed off to my new home of the next four years.

Following the instructions that the college sent, we drove for hours, switching from freeways to state highways then to city streets and finally turning onto what looked like a country road. As we got further and further away from civilization I grew more and more uneasy. When we finally reached the school it was so far from any town—much less a city—that I wondered how it could have looked so urban in the picture. I took out the brochure. Sure enough there were the three modern looking buildings as pictured, but what the brochure didn't show was that these were the *only* modern buildings on campus. Everything else looked like residential homes or forest reserve. There was so much nature and the campus was so quiet. I suppose that if I had been raised in an isolated hamlet in the Sierra Nevada mountains I might have found this place reminiscent of home. But being from a rather large Southern city I had wanted to go somewhere a little more cosmopolitan.

I lasted a semester before I went totally crazy. Then I transferred. This time I made sure that I visited the campuses and talked to students before I made a decision. It cost me a semester of happiness, but I had learned my lesson.

By: Aaron W. who is now a happy urban student at UCLA.

Many schools operate under a need-blind admissions policy. This means that they make their decisions without any reference to students' financial need. However, once you get accepted you can work with the college and the government to put together a financial aid package you can afford. Colleges and the government offer reasonable financial aid packages through a combination of grants, scholarships, work-study, and loans. Not until you are accepted by the college and they determine what kind of financial aid package they can offer will you need to worry about money. Check out Chapter 11: *How To Win Free Cash For College*, to see what kind of support is available and how you can maximize your aid package.

Remember, it is your future that we're talking about and you should think of college as an investment. (Hopefully you will have parents who feel the same and will be more than happy to foot the bill.)

Once you have decided where you are going to apply, you are ready to take the plunge into filling out the applications. So let's get started with the application form itself.

CREATE A STUNNING APPLICATION FORM

In This Chapter
▲ **Discover The Secrets Of The Application**
▲ **How To Beef Up & Prioritize Your Accomplishments**
▲ **Proper Application Form Style & Etiquette**
▲ **The "Correct" Way To Brag**
▲ **When To Leave Something Blank**
▲ **Chuck Out The White-Out Globs**

Write A Killer Application Form

We confess. The actual application form is hardly sexy. It lacks the challenge of the essay, the stress of the interview, and the personal touch of the evaluations. We won't deny that it is a pretty monotonous chore with a seemingly infinite number of questions, blanks, lines, and boxes.

But it is precisely for these reasons that many make careless mistakes and do not consider carefully how to strategically present their information. These deficiencies, while they may seem small, are often magnified in the eyes of the admissions officers and can take the edge off an otherwise perfect application.

You can think of your application form as your personal stats sheet, much like those of professional athletes. Instead of the number of rebounds or yards per run, your stats include test scores, years of participation in extracurricular activities, number of times you won a certain award, and, of course, your grades. The admissions officers use your application form as both a summary of your achievements and a way to quickly compare you to all the other applicants.

The goal of this chapter is to show you how even a little planning beforehand can not only save you time, but more important insure that your application truly stands out from the masses. (To get a true sense of the word "masses" try imagining the 23,000 applications that a school like UCLA gets each and every year!)

We will begin with some basic safety tips—that's right application forms require extra care since you usually have only one copy of the original. Then we'll look at format, style, and strategy. Be prepared to limber up those typing fingers and don't forget to keep a few bottles of white-out on hand.

Application Form Safety

If you think making photocopies of your application before filling it out is a waste of time, think again. We guarantee that at least half of your copies will get torn, smudged, or otherwise irrecoverably ruined by typos. For her Princeton application, one student we know went though 30 copies before she got it just right. (What would we do without our friend the photocopier?)

So, the first thing you should do is make five photocopies of each application form original. Then stash the originals in a safe place. Two of the copies will serve as your rough drafts and the rest will be extra copies in case you make an egregious error and need a new form.

Don't worry about sending the colleges copies of their application forms. They get thousands every year and don't care whether you send them back their originals or not.

It's Best To Be A Neat Freak

If you aren't a neat freak, try to pretend that you are. Otherwise you'll end up with a mountain of papers and brochures liable to take on a life of its own. You will be receiving numerous applications from various schools and they can easily become lost or misplaced if you're not careful. Here are a few quick and easy things you can do to keep yourself organized and efficient. First, get a binder or folder to house all the forms and brochures. Then on separate sheets of paper:

▶ List all of the colleges you are applying to and their deadlines. Check whether the applications must be postmarked by or received by the deadline. If an application must be *received* by the deadline, write down that application's deadline as one week before to allow for the time it takes to get there through the mail.

▶ Note if the school has a rolling admissions policy. Schools with rolling admissions policies admit and deny students as they receive their applications. When their class is full, they stop admitting. Thus, if the school employs rolling admissions, you will want to get your application in well before the deadline. The most selective schools usually do not use rolling admissions, but you should check to make sure.

▶ For each college, list all of the materials required. Don't forget: the actual application, fee, transcript, financial aid form, evaluations, school reports, mid-year school reports, standardized test score reports, self-addressed stamped envelopes, and postcards. This will insure that you won't forget any materials, which could delay the processing of your application. Keep these sheets with their respective applications.

Finally, keep each of your applications in a separate folder or envelope. As you complete an essay or finish a form you can easily dump it into the right envelope and won't risk any mix-ups. Do you know how many pieces of Harvard's application form get sent to Princeton by mistake? Well, let's just say that it happens more often than it should. Be careful.

Early Action And Early Decision: Signing Your Life Away

Okay, so you won't really sign your life away (we admit we wanted to attract your attention with a catchy headline), but you may have to commit to attending the college if you are accepted. These early bird specials in college admissions allow you to apply—as you may have guessed—earlier. Generally this means you must turn in your completed application and finish all of your testing by around November and you will receive notification in December or January.

The advantages of applying Early Action or Early Decision are that: 1) You demonstrate to the college that it is your top choice; and 2) You will find out sooner if you are accepted and thus may not have to apply elsewhere.

The disadvantages are that: 1) If you are deferred (neither accepted nor denied), your application may not be as favorably looked upon in the regular admissions process; and 2) For Early Decision, you are committed to attending that school if you are accepted and must withdraw your applications to all other schools. For Early Action, you don't have to make this commitment.

We suggest that you use these early bird specials, especially Early Decision, only if you are sure that the school is your first choice and you definitely want to go there. Otherwise, stick with the regular admissions schedule.

Get Friendly With A Typewriter Or Computer

Since your application form will be the first thing that the admissions officers look at and the first page in your file, it should be perfect. It must be typed neatly and free of spelling and grammatical errors. Severely crooked lines, using a prehistoric typewriter ribbon, or any other imperfection will certainly stand out (and not in a good way).

Typing (on a typewriter or computer) is required for the application forms. Although the instructions may say that it is alright to handwrite, you should always type. No matter how many neat handwriting awards you won in elementary school, nothing looks better or is easier to read than typewritten words. Colleges expect it, and nearly every other applicant whom you will be compared to will have typed their forms.

Make sure you choose a clear font and avoid printing using less than single spacing even if it means that you have to eliminate some things. We suggest using 10 to 12 point type.

Beef Up Your Extracurricular And Academic Life

The most important parts of the application form are the areas that make you shine. You can probably guess which parts these are: your extracurricular activities, jobs, and honors and awards (which we will discuss later). These are the sections that can really set you apart from other applicants. Anyone can take an English honors class, but not anyone can start an adult literacy program or become the manager at Wayne's Weenie World.

The first step is to make a list of all your extracurricular activities, summer activities, and jobs. List everything big and small. Significant and insignificant. Don't forget that extracurricular activities include experiences like teaching all those hyper kids at Sunday School, whacking the ball around on the ping pong team, playing the triangle in band, leading a sit-in against animal fur, or volunteering as a candy striper at the hospital.

For every activity, job, and sport you should try to list as much of the following as possible:

▶ Name of the organization, program, or business.

▶ A short one to two sentence description of the group, program, or business.

▶ Any leadership positions you held and your responsibilities.

▶ Any special projects that you initiated or oversaw. These could be either long-term or one-time projects.

▶ Dates you participated or worked.

▶ Number of hours per week you spent on the activity or job.

If you're having trouble remembering everything, make use of other people's memories. Although you are far from senility, you will still find that it is surprising what other people remember that you have overlooked. Show your list to your parents, teachers, siblings, friends, advisors, or anyone else who may recall something you did.

Leadership Is Better Than Membership

Let's have some fun and put on the shoes of an admissions officer for the next few paragraphs. Imagine that you are looking at your 551st and 552nd application for today. Whew, time to call it a day! But, before you go home, you need to make a decision about these last two. Here are some things that each mentioned in their list of activities.

Applicant A

1) Reporter for school newspaper
2) Speech team member
3) Young Voter Club Member

Applicant B

1) Editor-in-chief of school newspaper
2) Organizer of city-wide speech contest for 1,000 children
3) Director of Young Voter Registration for Democrat Club

Who would you admit? Of course Applicant B! The activities in which you have leadership roles or responsibility are the most memorable and impressive. Applicant B demonstrates her leadership and dedication through her accomplishments while Applicant A only catalogs his participation.

When describing your roles, do not be afraid to brag a little. You need to highlight the importance of your contributions and responsibilities. Admissions officers like to see students who are not only members but are also leaders. They want students who are initiators both inside and outside of the classroom.

Prioritize Your Activities

Now that you have your list, it's time to select which activities and jobs you are going to highlight and in what order. You probably will not have enough space to list everything, and even if you do you really only want to present those activities in which you made a contribution. You don't want to give the impression that you did a little of everything. Rather you want to emphasize the depth of your participation in a selection of activities.

Rank your activities in the order of importance based on those in which you were a leader or had responsibility. Even if you were not an officer in the club, if you elected to take charge of a special event or project you should note that on your list. After these come activities that are academic in nature as well as volunteer service.

How To Rank Your Activities And Jobs

To help you sort out which activities should come first you can use the following criteria to rank their significance: (Given in order of importance)

#1 Activities or businesses that you initiated or founded. These should always be listed first.

#2 Activities in which you were the leader—president, vice president, or captain—or jobs in which you oversaw others. Even if the form does not provide a space, note your title or responsibilities (e.g., Smithtown Public Library—Children's Reading Program Coordinator).

#3 Activities in which you held a lesser position like secretary, treasurer, etc.

#4 Activities or jobs in which you made a special contribution (don't forget to note that contribution in a few words) or sports in which you have excelled.

#5 Activities of academic importance. (e.g., National Honor Society Member) and public service.

#6 Activities with impressive sounding names (e.g., International Association of Shockwave Enhanced World Wide Web Page Publishers) and sports in which you do not particularly excel.

#7 Everything else.

Keep in mind the dates of your participation. If possible you want to include activities that span all four years so that you present a consistent pattern of participation.

Depending on how much space you have you also want to add some diversity. If your top five activities are all related to your passion for calculus, you may want to throw in your membership on the cross country team (even if you are a terrible runner) just to show that you are interested in more than quadratic equations.

Here's an example of an application form in which you are given only a small amount of space:

PLEASE LIST YOUR EXTRACURRICULAR AND VOLUNTEER ACTIVITIES

Student Council President (12th); Class President (9th); NHS secretary (12th); Big Brothers Volunteer (9th-present); Key Club Volunteer Tutor (10th); Tennis Team (9th-11th); Band (9th).

Here's an example of a more generous application that gives you more room to explain:

PLEASE LIST YOUR EXTRACURRICULAR AND VOLUNTEER ACTIVITIES

President, Student Council—chairs monthly meetings, serves on district council, initiated and organizes Toys for Tots donation drive, founded and maintains student concerns feedback system, oversaw implementation of revised student constitution. (12th grade).

Secretary, National Honor Society—publishes monthly minutes, serves on fund-raising committee, established and maintains World Wide Web homepage, chairs new members selection committee. (12th grade).

Volunteer, Big Brothers & Sisters—meets twice each week to tutor little brother at Oaks Elementary School; teaches basic math, reading, and composition. (9th-present).

Varsity Tennis Team—first singles player; placed 2nd in district in 10th grade and 4th in state in 11th grade. Organized school's first "Charity Tennis Tournament." (9th-present).

Bragging Rights From Your Honors And Awards

Do you remember how your mother would react when your Aunt April started going off about how precious your two highly competitive cousins were and how they were being showered with praise from their teachers? If your mother was like ours, she would probably have started firing back her own barrage, cataloging every award you had won since the 3rd grade in alphabetical order: Aardvark Lover of the Year, Boy Scouts of America Volunteer Award, Certificate of Merit for the Science Fair...

When it comes to writing about your honors and awards in your applications, you should take on the persona of your proud mother. Brag about your accomplishments as if you are proving that you are indisputably better than your cousins (which you already know is true).

Just as when listing activities, there are guidelines for determining which awards and honors to list first. Start with awards that carry the most weight, such as national or state recognition. After that, awards that very few get or that are highly prized in your school or community. Academic awards of any kind should be high on your list followed by awards for leadership, community service, club activities, and athletics.

When listing the award, highlight its significance by stating how many received the award each year or for each region. The words, "one awarded each year," or "one award per district" emphasize the importance of the honor. For example, it's impressive if you won an award for your commitment to community service; but it's even more impressive if you note that only one student from each school receives such recognition.

You should also add explanations for those awards with titles that are not immediately recognizable. For example, "Stallion Award Recipient" could be an award for academic achievement, community service, or excellence in horse breeding. Make sure what the award is for is clear.

Here's an example of a well ordered, yet concise summary of an applicant's honors and awards:

ACADEMIC HONORS
Briefly describe any scholastic distinctions or honors you have won since the 9th grade:

1st Place Oratory: State Speech Tournament (12th); Outstanding Junior: 1 awarded/year (11th); 2nd Place Research: Science Fair (11th); 1st Place Creative Writing Contest: 2 per grade (11th); Principal's List (9th-present); Certificate: French Class (10th).

Make A Name For Yourself As An Author

There is nothing more exciting than seeing your name in print as an author (we know from experience). This is an impressive achievement that can help your application stand out. However, most application forms don't have spaces to list published works.

If you do not have enough jobs to fill up the occupations section, you may want to list your published works there with "author" as the job title. Write the title of your work and where and when it was published in the rest of the space. You can also list publications in either the extracurricular activities or honors and awards section depending on where you have space.

Time To Start Typing

Now that you know what you want to say, it's time to say it. With your prioritized list in front of you, take out one photocopy of an application form and handwrite your answers to all the questions. This way when you are ready to type, you will have all the information you need and will not have to stop each time you need to find an answer, date, or other detail. (This little time saving shortcut really adds up after doing five or six applications.)

Once you have completed this, take another copy and type a draft of your answers to test the spacing. Most likely you will find that some of your answers are too long when typed and will need to be shortened. You may also find that you have some extra space and can afford to add a few more descriptive sentences.

Try to use all of the space given. Be careful, however, not to cram in too much by using a small font or very close spacing. Admissions officers tend to have tired eyes (you would too after reading several thousand applications) and will not tolerate type that they cannot easily read. Use your last copies for the real thing. Never use the original form. Remember Murphy's Law: Anything that can go wrong will and at the worst possible moment.

When To Leave Things Blank

Application forms are not like art: White space is not aesthetically pleasing. If you do not have enough activities to fill all the spaces, then try adding more description to those that you are listing. This way you not only expand on those activities which are impressive but you also minimize the white space. It is perfectly valid to substitute quality for quantity.

Don't be afraid to reach back into the past and list a few things you did during your freshman year. Revealing that you were a member of the Square Dancing Squad adds an interesting and heartwarming personal touch—especially if you went on to become a 250 pound nose guard for the football team.

One warning: If you really have no other significant contributions to list, resist the temptation to fill your form with meaningless information. It is better to leave a few blanks than to write about how you donated a can of tuna to the holiday food drive. Those activities that lack significance will only reveal your desperation to fill up the space and will make the admissions officer question your ability to gauge importance.

Most likely you will find that you don't have enough space. Often you will have to make some difficult choices and not include some important activities. Try to creatively shorten your long sentences, which happens to be the topic of the next section.

Nip And Tuck In All The Right Places

The limited space on the application form will force you to rely on your most creative skills of manipulation. Most students find that the spaces on the application forms are hardly wide enough for a single sentence let alone a complete description of their activities from the past four years. The key is to be clear, yet concise, by nipping and tucking wherever possible. For example, you should not write:

As vice president of the National Honor Society I helped to run a canned food drive to benefit a local charity.

Instead write:

National Honor Society (VP). Organized charity food drive.

This second sentence is concise, to the point, and much stronger than the first example.

If the application form provides only a small box into which you must list your activities you should list the important ones first, include your leadership positions in parentheses, and separate the activities with semicolons. For example:

Smith High Recycling Coalition (Founder); NHS (Pres.); Student Council (VP); Math Club (Meet Organizer); BSA (Eagle Scout).

You can often abbreviate activities that are nationally recognized or well-known among educators. There are some schools brimming with generosity that allow you to use extra sheets. You should take advantage of the gift of space but remember that economy of words is important. Admissions officers don't have the time to read excessive explanations.

Chuck Out The White-Out Globs

This may seem obvious, but you would be surprised at how many applications are written in illegible handwriting or are caked with globs of white-out. We have already advised against handwriting, but even when you type your application you need to be careful about excessive white-out.

A few corrections are fine, but the more white-out you use and the messier your application, the more distracted the admissions officers will be by your mistakes. And trust us, you do not want them to start counting the number of mistakes you made throughout your application.

The best way to correct errors (aside from not making them) is to use a correcting typewriter or a computer program for filling out forms. But, whichever way you correct your typos never use a pen to add a letter to a misspelled word or X's to cross out an entire word or line of text. If the mistake is that pronounced, you should retype the entire application form. (Remember our advice about making plenty of extra copies.)

When filling out the form, you need to devote your full attention to its accuracy. It's truly amazing how easy it is to mistype something. One unsuccessful Yale applicant actually typed the name of the college with a "T" instead of "Y." Unfortunately he discovered this mistake after he had already mailed off the application. Pay close attention to what you are doing and no matter how tempting, never type while watching TV.

Leave No Question Unanswered

Check and double-check to make sure that you have filled in every blank and checked every box. In the spaces that are not applicable to you, type a dash so that you know that you have not left the space blank by mistake. If your form is incomplete, it could be returned to you and will certainly reflect poorly on your attention to detail.

Finally... Don't Forget To Sign

One last thing before you put the application aside: Do not forget to autograph it in all the right places. There are probably several forms that require your signature, and without it your application will *not* be processed.

HOW TO GET THE RIGHT EVALUATIONS

● ●

In This Chapter
- ▲ How To Hunt Down The Best Recommenders
- ▲ How To Get Great Evaluations
- ▲ Playing The Name Game
- ▲ The Perfect Cover Letter
- ▲ Our Secret Fail-Safe Weapon For Excellent Evaluations
- ▲ Stories From Real Life: How My Recommender Cost Me $5,000

Find Someone To Brag About You

If there is one skill that you will hone throughout the admissions process it will be the art of tasteful bragging. You may, for example, have already described your job flipping burgers as that of a "culinary coordinator." Or your part-time baby-sitting for the next door neighbor as training in "human education, development, and discipline distribution."

The evaluations and school report are a slight modification of this bragging rite. This time you will be entrusting others, like your teachers and counselors, to sing your praises.

Evaluations are highly valued by admissions officers for the insight they provide into who you are. They rely on them to learn about your personality, skills, ambitions, and weaknesses. It's not that they don't trust you, but they want proof in the form of what other people say that you really are as terrific as you say.

Your mission, which you have no choice but to accept, is to provide them with this proof. Although you do not have direct control over what your recommenders write, there is plenty that you can do to insure that your evaluations will present only your best points. And this will hopefully be the last confirmation that the admissions officers need to offer you admission.

Start Early

Most colleges require two teacher evaluations and a school report completed by your counselor, principal, or headmaster. Some schools also allow you to submit an extra evaluation. Giving out the evaluation forms early should be your first priority.

Recommenders need at least three weeks if not several months to prepare your evaluations, especially if they are busy teachers or administrators and have a stack of other evaluations to write. Before doing anything else, work on distributing the forms to them. Refer to the *Do The Grunt Work For Your Recommenders* section in this chapter to learn how to put together a complete packet for each of your recommenders. But first, you will need to find some recommenders.

Hunt Down The Best Recommenders

Identifying quality recommenders is much like finding star witnesses for a courtroom. You want people who can testify in support of your strengths, who are believable, and who won't reveal anything incriminating. Essentially you want to find people who know your strengths and will attest to them.

For example, if your English teacher thinks that you are the next Hemingway, then you should ask him. Or, if biology is so easy that your teacher asks you to grade the exams, then you should ask her. Obviously the teachers in whose classes you excel will be your most likely candidates.

For the school report, you may not have a choice who to ask. Many colleges specify which administrator should complete the report, usually your counselor, college advisor, principal, or schoolmaster. If you are given a choice, of course pick the one who knows you and your accomplishments best.

The Bonus Evaluation

Some colleges are incredibly generous and offer you the opportunity to submit a third evaluation. Take them up on it. Even if they don't offer, you may want to do it anyway as long as you know of a good recommender.

You can assume that many applicants to selective colleges will be top students and have decent evaluations from their teachers. A third evaluation can help you stand out from these applicants. Your two teacher evaluations will show that you have the intellectual mettle; a third evaluation can speak about your character or a special talent or interest that you have. As you know, colleges are very interested in attracting well-rounded students. In fact, the reason some colleges ask for a third evaluation is so that you can show them just how "round" you are.

Just like your teacher evaluations, you want to select a third recommender who knows you well. It should be someone who can describe a unique talent or interest that you have. A couple of our suggestions are your activity advisor, work supervisor, volunteer supervisor, church leader, or coach. But remember that if you don't have an extra person who can write an excellent evaluation then it is better not to dilute your two or three terrific recommendations with a so-so extra.

Get Recommenders Who Can Write About The Intimate Details Of Your Life

If you approach a teacher and ask him to write your evaluation, and he responds, "What's your name again?" that's a hint that he's not the one for you.

You want recommenders who can write about the specifics of your life, providing personal anecdotes and examples if possible. Only people who know you well can refer to specific incidents and even provide humorous stories that not only lend a genuineness to their evaluations but also make them memorable. College admissions officers will read thousands of evaluations, and for yours

The Best Evaluations Are From The Heart

One of the most sincere evaluations we've read was written by a 9-year-old child whom Linda G., a high school senior, befriended at a local shelter for battered women. Patti, whose mother had recently left her abusive husband, wrote about the high school student, who spent two afternoons each week with her.—Authors

Dear college,

My name is Patti and I am 9 years old. I am writing to tell you about my best friend Linda. When I first came to the shelter I was scared and embarrassed. My father hurt my mother. At first my mother never smiled or laughed. Linda changed that. She was very nice to me and played with me. We played tag and dolls and other games. She always made me laugh and my mother laugh, too, with her jokes.

Every time I say good-bye to her, she gives me a very big hug. She tells me that I am smart and pretty and that I am going to go to college someday. At first I didn't believe her. My family is poor. My mother didn't go to college. But Linda has told me so many times that I do believe her. I want to be just like her. I want to get good grades and become a doctor, too. And I want to make my mother laugh and smile like Linda does every time she visits us. I want to be just like Linda.

Patti

Coupled with an evaluation from the director of the shelter as well as two evaluations from her teachers, Linda's recommenders presented a vivid and heartwarming portrait of a dedicated person who is deeply involved in community service and wants to help make a difference. Since she chose to emphasize her extracurricular involvement with the shelter throughout her application (Linda's essay was about Patti's mother), the letter from Patti was both appropriate and effective. Linda successfully showed that beyond the scores and transcripts she is a motivated, hard working, and genuinely caring person who would bring such desirable qualities to any college campus.

Of course, this does not mean that you should rush out and start volunteering just so you can find a child to write you a nice letter, but it does mean that you should consider submitting an extra evaluation from someone who can highlight and emphasize other areas of strength. And this someone does not have to be a teacher.

to stand out, it needs to be written in a way that is different from the rest.

The sad fact is that most students pick recommenders who do not know them well enough. Even if a teacher gave you an "A+," you may not necessarily want an evaluation from her especially if you did not have the chance to get to know her. In high school many teachers may give you "A's" (we hope all), but only a few really know you well enough to be able to cite specifics.

An evaluation from a teacher who does not know you well but who gave you a good grade will certainly contain such generic compliments as "So-and-so is a fine student," or "So-and-so is great at such-and-such subject." These phrases, however, will appear in almost every other applicant's evaluation as well. Such evaluations are of little value in helping you to stand out.

Only a handful of evaluations, those from recommenders who know the student, will contain such unforgettable phrases as, "So-and-so is not only the best English student I have had but has nearly doubled the readership of our literary magazine," or "So-and-so wrote an article on drug use in our school that was the talk of the town for months." These statements, which when supported by vivid details, will be the ones that admissions officers will not be able to forget.

Whenever possible, you should try to select a good combination of recommenders who can praise your academic, extracurricular, and leadership-motivational abilities. Let's take a look at such an example.

Tom, a student who was accepted at both Princeton and Berkeley, had two high school teachers and a student council advisor write evaluations. However, in addition to writing about his academic achievements his teachers were also able to comment on his involvement in groups that they advised, namely the speech team and the school newspaper. Thus, while Tom's teacher evaluations provided solid evidence of his scholastic aptitude, they also showed his other interests and abilities. A third evaluation from his student council advisor completed the picture of Tom as an all-around outstanding student by describing his contributions to the school community.

The Name Game: Bigger Isn't Always Better

You might think that the best evaluation you can have is one from a person with high name value, like the President of the United States. After all, what college would reject someone recommended by the nation's leader, right?

The problem with this logic is this: Do you know the President or any other public official or famous person well enough that he or she can write about you in a personal and detailed way? (If the answer is "yes," then by all means take advantage of your connection.) If the answer is "no," then it really doesn't matter what title your recommender has unless he or she can write a meaningful and individual letter.

We had a friend named David who selected people solely on the basis of their name value. He was able to get evaluations from the school principal, a district superintendent, and the lieutenant governor for whom he had served as a summer intern but only met once. While the lieutenant governor's name may have initially attracted attention, the evaluation itself, David discovered, was a photocopied form letter with his name handwritten in the blank. And as if that were not bad enough, the letter contained typos!

The only time a famous person will do you any good is if he or she really knows you well. If your governor is better known to you as Uncle Pete, then use your connections. But if he wouldn't recognize you walking down the street, then don't chance asking a mere acquaintance with a good name. As David's stack of rejections proved, it's much better to get people who actually know you than those with impressive titles.

A Final Note About Numbers

We know of an applicant who once sent 10 evaluations even though the college only asked for 3. She thought that the more testimonials verifying her abilities, the better. However, sending 10 evaluations was excessive and probably caused more annoyance than awe. When colleges specify a certain number of evalua-

Stories From Real Life Stories From Real Life Stories From Real Life

How My U.S. Senator Used My Evaluation As A Political Platform

When I was selected for a summer internship to work for my state's longest serving and most respected U.S. Senator, I had grand dreams of personally advising him about new legislation and discussing politics over business lunches. I thought that I had just won a free ride into college. After all, what more prestigious summer job could a student have than to work for a national leader?

On the first day of the internship my dreams were pretty much shattered. I found out from his secretary that he wouldn't even be in the state for the next two months and that none of the interns had ever privately dined with the Senator. I spent my summer sending out photographs that were signed not by the Senator but by one of his four automated signature machines.

On the last day of my internship I met him for the first time. He held a luncheon to thank all of the summer interns. My only contact with him was shaking his hand as he said to me, "Thank you for your help." Still, I thought it was incredible to cross the path of such a great man. When I applied to college, I was ecstatic that the Senator's secretary said he would write an evaluation. What more would the colleges need than an endorsement from a national hero, leader, and role model?

The Senator's secretary sent me copies of the evaluation for my applications and an extra one for my records. Since the evaluation was not intended to be confidential I opened my copy. It was the worst evaluation that I had ever seen!

In the first paragraph it stated generically that I had been a good intern who worked hard. However, the rest of the evaluation read more like a political speech and outlined how the Senator wished that more students were interested in politics, how the future of the country relied on the education of current students, and how pursuing higher education was a noble cause. While this was all true and it said a lot about the Senator's stand on education and America's youth, it said almost nothing about me, which was supposed to be the point of the evaluation.

Needless to say, I quickly asked for an evaluation from my math teacher, whose platform was not political lobbying but rather lobbying to get me into college. And I was very pleased with the results.

By: Chris O. who has vowed not to volunteer for any more politicians.

Stories From Real Life Stories From Real Life Stories From Real Life

tions, you should not exceed this number, unless you have the most extraordinary evaluation ever lined up.

Too many evaluations submitted under the theory that strength can be achieved in numbers will actually weaken the overall impact of your evaluations. If you have three teachers who will write great evaluations and a former boss who will write an average recommendation, do not include the average recommendation. "Strength in numbers" does not work for college evaluations.

Once you have identified two or three people who can write sincerely about you and your strong points, the next step is to insure that they write good evaluations. If you have picked your recommenders well and follow the ensuing points, it should be easy. Plus, we have included our *Secret Fail-Safe Weapon For Excellent Evaluations* for you to use at the end of this chapter.

Avoid Busy Crunch Times

When asking recommenders to write an evaluation it is important that you approach them at an appropriate time. The best times are when they are not busy and, if possible, when they are alone. Explain that you are applying to college and that you would like them to write an evaluation. Ask them if they think they will be able to complete the evaluation by the deadline.

If your potential recommender does not have time, don't curse him or her, fear that you have no hope of getting in, or take it personally. It is very likely that he or she is simply too busy, and an evaluation written in haste would surely not improve your chances of getting accepted anyway.

If your recommenders agree to write the evaluations, tell them that you will give them a packet with all of the necessary information. And don't forget to thank them profusely.

Do The Grunt Work For Your Recommenders

Once you have found your recommenders you should prepare a packet of all the materials they will need to write detailed and complete evaluations. These packets will take some time to organize, but they will make your recommenders' job much easier and will ultimately help them to write better evaluations. These packets should include the following:

#1 **Cover Letter.** The letter should explain what wonderful things you want your recommenders to emphasize. Cite specific examples and accomplishments. Remember that your teachers and counselors have known many students, which means they probably won't remember what you did last semester let alone two years ago. You need to remind them of all the great things you have done!

The letter should also clearly state the schools you are applying to and their deadlines. Don't forget to thank recommenders in advance for their time and effort. Take a look at the sample cover letter in the following section.

#2 **Resume.** Include a resume that gives detailed information about appropriate activities, jobs, and academic achievements. This will be a valuable reference for your recommenders, refreshing their memories about what you have accomplished. (You can also include a copy with your applications to the colleges.)

Take the time to tailor your resume for each of your recommenders so that it emphasizes the information that pertains to him or her. For example, for your math teacher, you would emphasize and list your math coursework and grades as well as all of the various math awards you received before you list your extracurricular activities. For an advisor of a public service club, however, you would highlight your contributions to the club and include information about your other public service work, placing less emphasis on all those math awards.

#3 **The Evaluation Forms.** *← Part of the Common App.* You should complete the waivers and basic information portions before giving the forms to your recommenders. Although you might have ideological objections to signing away your right to see these evaluations, you should do so anyway. Colleges realize that when recommenders know that their evaluations will remain confidential they will write more honestly. A great evaluation in which the applicant refuses to sign away his or her right to see it does not carry as much weight as one in which the applicant has made it known to the recommender that the evaluation will forever remain confidential.

#4 **Secret Fail-Safe Weapon For Excellent Evaluations.** This is an article at the end of the chapter which you should give to your recommenders. It will give them valuable tips on how to write an effective and personalized evaluation.

#5 **Mailing Envelopes.** Be polite enough to attach the correct amount of postage for your recommenders to send the evaluations to the schools. Also, don't forget to address the envelopes.

By the way, these packets of material, while a pain to make for each recommender, will have the additional effect of showing your recommenders how organized you are and will remind them of how important you consider their evaluations to be.

The Perfect Cover Letter

Be sure that the cover letter you include in your packet to each evaluator contains the following:

#1 The importance of the evaluation and what wonderful things you would like them to write about you. Be as specific as you can about what you would like the evaluation to include, providing examples and accomplishments to which your recommenders may refer. There is nothing wrong with helping your recommenders with their letter. In fact, they will be happy that you did!

#2 Instructions on what they should do after they finish their evaluations. Provide them with envelopes already addressed to the correct office at each college. Also, request that your recommenders make a copy of their evaluations in case for some catastrophic reason, they are lost in the mail. ← *I always do this, even though they are saved in my computer.*

#3 The schools to which you are applying and their deadlines.

#4 Your heartfelt appreciation for them taking time from their busy schedule to help you.

The following is a sample cover letter to a teacher:

Dear Mrs. Chandler,

Thank you again for agreeing to write an evaluation. As you know, I am applying to eight colleges, and each of the evaluations you write is a very important part of my application. The colleges will use the evaluations to get a better idea of who I am beyond my test scores and grades so the more detailed and personal you can make the evaluation, of course, the better.

In your evaluation, I would appreciate it if you would write about my performance in your economics class, especially about the mock stock market project I led. The project gave me the opportunity to apply what we learned from our textbook and lectures toward a semester long activity in which the entire class participated. It also made me consider pursuing a degree in economics in college.

I would also appreciate it if you would describe my tenure as President of the Business Club, especially noting how we worked to build membership and increase sales during our annual candy sale. You may recall my leadership in reviving the club's newsletter and in organizing our annual conference. With your evaluation and those from my history teacher, Mr. Bing, and my work supervisor at the library, I hope the colleges will get a better picture of who I am.

I am also including a copy of my resume and a short article that I found addressed to recommenders which I thought you might find interesting since I'm sure you must be flooded with requests. When you are finished with my evaluations you can mail them directly to the colleges in the pre-addressed envelopes that I have enclosed.

Thank you again for your time and effort. I am listing below the colleges to which I am applying and the deadlines for the evalua-tions. The colleges also recommend that you make a copy of the evaluations, as they have been known in rare cases to get lost in the mail. If you have any questions, please do not hesitate to ask.

Harvard University (deadline)   Penn State (deadline)
Stanford University (deadline)   Princeton University (deadline)
U.C. Berkeley (deadline)   U. Penn. (deadline)
U.C. Irvine (deadline)   University of Washington (deadline)

Sincerely yours,

Notice how the cover letter accomplishes a number of things in a short space. It explains the purpose of the evaluations, de-scribes what the recommender should focus on, reminds her of past accomplishments as well as gives specific examples which she can use, clearly lays out the deadlines, and thanks her profusely. All of these are essential elements of the cover letter and will result in your recommenders writing much better evaluations.

Be A Frequent Visitor To Your Recommenders

You don't have to blare a message over the school loudspeaker to remind your recommenders of their responsibility, but you do need to make sure that they finish your evaluations before the deadline. You cannot assume that a recommender, regardless of how responsible he or she usually is, will finish your evaluations on time.

What this means is that you must devise some tactful ways to ask your recommenders if they have finished your evaluations before the deadline. You don't want to harass them, but you do want to gently check, well before any due dates, the progress of your evaluations.

One way is to see your recommenders more often than usual. Reroute your walk home so that you pass by the restaurant where you worked last summer, and drop by and visit your previous science teacher once a week. Have a couple of questions for your teacher, giving you an excuse to strike up a conversation. While talking, tell them how busy you have been with your applications. Maybe even ask for some advice on your essay.

In any case make sure you ask them if they have any questions about your evaluations. Suggest that you can provide more biographical information or a more detailed resume if they need one. They will probably decline your offer but will usually tell you how they are progressing.

As the deadlines approach for the evaluations, thank them again for spending the time to write them—hopefully they will tell you that they have already finished. If, however, the deadline is fast approaching and they still haven't gotten their act together, then you will need to directly remind them of the impending deadlines. You do not want to badger your recommenders, but you do want to make sure that they submit your evaluations on time.

How My Recommender Cost Me $5,000

Although college evaluations are the subject, scholarship evaluations also have deadlines that are equally important as the following example reveals.—Authors

When I was in college, I applied for a scholarship from a national journalism organization of which I was a member. The previous year I was a runner-up for the $5,000 prize, and the scholarship committee informed me that the only reason why I didn't win was because I had only two years experience working for non-school newspapers, and I found out from friends on the committee that I would basically be a shoo-in for the following year's competition.

I applied again the following year after having completed a summer internship with *The Washington Post* and a term-time internship with *Newsweek*. With these two experiences, I was positive that I would win the competition this time. The application required an essay, newspaper clips, and three evaluations. I submitted the essay and clips directly and contacted three of my previous employers at various newspapers to write evaluations. All three agreed.

About two weeks after the deadline, I received a letter from the scholarship committee. I opened it expecting to find a congratulatory notice. Excitement quickly changed to horror as I read the letter which stated that my application had been deemed incomplete and had therefore been disqualified.

I immediately called the scholarship committee to find out what had happened. Did I forget to submit my essay? Had I left blank a critical part of the application form? As it turned out my application was complete except for one small detail: A recommender had not submitted an evaluation. I begged and pleaded with the scholarship representative to allow my delinquent recommender to fax in the evaluation that day. The person, of course, said, "No." It was too late.

For several days I moped around, cursing my recommender for costing me the $5,000 prize. That was a lot of money to lose over a single evaluation! In retrospect I realize that although it was my recommender who had forgotten, it was also my fault for not having reminded her. If I would have just made one simple phone call, I would have avoided being disqualified. It was an expensive lesson that cost me five grand. Please don't make the same mistake.

By: Jeanne T. who now follows up with all of her recommenders.

Make Your Recommenders Feel Warm And Fuzzy

Another subtle way of reminding your recommenders to fin-ish their evaluations on time is by writing them thank you letters right before the deadlines. This way, your recommenders will get one of the best reminders possible—one that assumes that they have already done what they said they were going to do even if they haven't.

Thank your recommenders for their time and effort, and ex-plain what an important role they have played in your pursuit of higher education. If you feel it is appropriate, give them a small thank you gift. Keep them posted throughout the process, and tell them to which schools you are accepted.

Our Secret Fail-Safe Weapon For Excellent Evaluations

As promised in the beginning of this chapter, the following is a fail-safe weapon to insure that your recommenders write evalua-tions that will stand out and really draw attention to your applica-tion. It is especially important when using recommenders who do not have experience with writing college evaluations and who, while sincere in their desire to help you, may not know about the special requirements of college evaluations.

Include the following article with your packet to your recommenders. Tell your recommenders that you thought the ar-ticle might be helpful in explaining how their evaluations will be used by the colleges.

Now Get Started!

That's it for how to get good evaluations. Now the only thing left to do is to hand out those forms early!

Evaluating The Evaluation

Tips From One Teacher's Encounter With The Truth About College Evaluations

By: Dr. Dale White

From *Get Into Any College: Secrets Of Harvard Students.* Available from 101 Publishing, 4546 B10 El Camino Real, Suite 281, Los Altos, CA 94022. Copyright 1997. Reproduction for commercial purposes or distribution is strictly prohibited without the prior written permission of the publisher.

As an English teacher at a rather elite private high school in New Hampshire I could always count on two things in the fall: the stunningly beautiful changing of the leaves and the endless requests from my seniors to write evaluations for college. Since I wrote between 50 and 60 evaluations a year, I had developed a rather efficient system.

I had five types of ranked form letters stored on my computer, and each corresponded to my assessment of the student. The letters had a blank space for the student's name and a few areas where I could add specific comments about grades and performance. Most of my students got letter Type 2 or Type 3 and only a few got letter Type 1, which I reserved for my best students.

For all except my top students I spent only about 10 to 15 minutes on each evaluation, and that included changing the paper in the printer to the school's letterhead. All in all I was very satisfied with my system and never once thought about what happened to the letters once they were dropped into the mail.

Last year this self-confidence was shattered. In the fall I returned to my university to pursue an advanced degree in education. For one of my classes I had chosen to write about college admissions and made arrangements to watch the admissions process firsthand.

I was put in touch with one of the senior admissions officers whose job was to read through the second cut of applications. All of the applications that passed his desk had survived previous evaluations by other officers. This officer, whom I will call Mr. B, was a career administrator and had done his job for nearly 15 years. Needless to say he was quite the expert.

The first thing that struck me about Mr. B's office was the huge stacks of applications that he had to review. There must have been hundreds of folders, each representing one applicant—and this was after the first cut. As Mr. B opened the first folder, I was curious to see what materials he would focus on. Of course, the essay was important, and Mr. B quickly read over the ones whose applications were promising.

But what surprised me the most was the time he spent on the evaluations. I was shocked to find that after looking very carefully at each of the evaluations, Mr. B would occasionally take a highlighter and mark certain passages.

I asked him why he highlighted only a few of the passages and if this meant the recommender had written something negative about the applicant. Mr. B looked at me, sighed, and told me that the highlighted passages were actually signs of a good recommendation.

He continued to explain that more than 90% of the evaluations he sees are generic, and when he finds one that is unique or mentions something that distinguishes the applicant from the hundreds he has already read, he marks it with his highlighter. According to Mr. B, who can read as many as 300 evaluations a day, unless he takes the effort to mark the few good ones, he cannot really tell the difference between the first evaluation he reads and the last.

Mr. B emphasized that he and his colleagues highly value evaluations that tell them something specific about the applicant. Unfortunately what he and other admissions officers end up reading are mostly canned compliments. Mr. B even recited from memory the top ten most common phrases that he encountered. Included were some that I had used in evaluations of my own students. Phrases like "Mr. Y is a great student and highly motivated." Or, "Ms. K is a thoughtful and outgoing person." Or, "Mr. A is a highly capable student and will be an outstanding freshman at your school." How many of us teachers have used such adjectives to describe students who we truly admired?

The plain truth is that admissions officers like Mr. B receive thousands of evaluations and after reading evaluation after evaluation, most begin to sound very similar and do nothing to help an applicant's chance of getting accepted. After talking to Mr. B and seeing which evaluations he considered to be truly effective, I decided to come up with a short list of tips which I hope will be of use. The following are four things to remember when writing a good evaluation:

1. Be Specific. The best evaluations contain specific examples of what the student has accomplished. If you say the student is a "real leader in school," then be sure to back up your statement with a solid example. Describe how he or she single-handedly organized the Culture Fair or how he or she led students in a petition to increase funding for the arts program. Now I ask students who request an evaluation from me to provide me with a resume and, if necessary, a short essay on what they have accomplished to help refresh my memory.

2. Write About The Student As An Individual. Remember that although you must comment on the student's academic accomplishments and/or extracurricular activities, the colleges also want to know what kind of person they might be getting. So mention something positive about the student's character or background. For example, if your school is in an area that is economically disadvantaged and few students even dream of going go to college, then mention this fact and comment on how hard the student has worked to break free from this cycle. Such background information on the student's community will help to establish a memorable picture of him or her and will help to set his or her accomplishments in the proper context.

3. Never List. The worst evaluations simply list accomplishments, regurgitating the information on the student's resume. "Mr. A was president of his class in his sophomore year. The following year he was the band leader, etc." These evaluations are boring and redundant. The student will already have listed his or her coursework, scores, awards, and extracurricular activities in the application.

While you should make reference to the student's accomplishments, try to expand and add detail from your point of view. Be sure to comment on extracurricular activities with which you are familiar. If you are the student's English teacher and journalism advisor then comment on his or her performance and involvement with the newspaper. This is the kind of evaluation that can only come from you and will help your student's chances immensely.

4. Proofread Your Evaluation. Innocent misspellings and errors in grammar not only make you look bad but also detract from the entire quality of your evaluation, which will ultimately hurt the student whom you are trying to help. Colleges expect applicants to submit near perfect applications and expect the same for the evaluations. It's surprising how many evaluations from teachers contain gross spelling and grammatical errors.

The importance of your role as evaluator cannot be emphasized enough. In fact, Mr. B showed me a copy of an evaluation from several years ago that he said was almost single-handedly responsible for getting an applicant into college. While I cannot reprint this evaluation, I can tell you that it was extremely well-written, very personal, and painted a picture of the applicant so vivid that you felt as if you had already met her. While the evaluations that you write for your students are part of a larger process, they can have a tremendous effect on the chances of their being admitted.

I hope the information in this short article will be of help when you write your evaluations. As for me, I have erased all of my ready-made evaluations and now exclusively write from scratch. It takes longer, but the evaluations are much better. I also insist that students give me a list of their accomplishments and even help to refresh my memory on the specific things they have done. All of this makes for better evaluations, and the ultimate reward for me as a teacher is for my students to come to class in the spring with big smiles on their faces and letters of acceptance in their hands.

- letters on his businesses -
dog walking + gardening
— be specific —

HOW TO WRITE AN
IRRESISTIBLE ESSAY

In This Chapter
- ▲ Why The Essay Is King
- ▲ The 5 Step Workshop To Writing Winning Essays
- ▲ Essay-Writing Absolute "Don'ts" That You Must Know
- ▲ The Super List Of Totally Dumb Topics
- ▲ Vital Tips For Specific Questions

The Essay: King Of The Application

You can have ho-hum grades and still get into Harvard. You can have average SAT scores and still get into Berkeley. You can even have mediocre teacher evaluations and still get into Princeton. But the one thing that spells instant rejection from any college is a poorly written essay. The essay is one of the most important parts of your application, and as you will discover, it is also the most difficult. Fortunately, the essay is also the area you have the most control over and can improve dramatically by following the strategies and tips outlined in this chapter.

The Essay In The Eyes Of The Admissions Officer

An Ivy League admissions officer once told us that of all the parts of the application, the most memorable and important is the essay. This 12-year veteran of the college admissions process explained that while each section of the application is carefully considered by the admissions committee, it is only the essay that has the potential to make or break an applicant's chance of getting accepted.

Why is the essay so important? Quite simply because it is viewed by admissions officers as their window into the "real" you. While thousands of applicants have similar test scores, grades, evaluations, and extracurricular activities; it is the essay that gives your application that all-important personal touch.

Through your essay the admissions officers hear your voice and see how you respond to questions or problems. Your essay is representative of you, and because colleges are interested in admitting interesting and thoughtful human beings—not just students with certain numerical scores—the essay is an indispensable resource for them.

The essay also shows the admissions officers your writing ability. It is no secret that some students at Harvard have been admitted with mediocre grades, SAT scores, or evaluations simply because they have written essays so extraordinary that the admissions officers were willing to overlook their other shortcomings.

All Questions Can Be Answered In Exactly The Same Way

We know of several applicants who applied to more than 25 schools. Unless you have nothing better to do with your time and money than apply to colleges, (which we hope is not the case) this is certainly overkill.

However, even if you apply to only one-third as many schools, you still may feel a little distressed at having to write two or three essays for each school. If you are applying to 10 schools this could translate into tens of thousands of words to write. Since each school will probably ask you to write on a slightly different question, you may wonder if you will have to compose 10 or 15 different essays. The answer, thankfully, is no. With a technique called "recycling" you should not have to write more than a few major essays regardless of how many schools to which you are applying.

The truth is that the question or topic of the essay is really only a guideline. It is designed to give you something concrete about which to write. Therefore, you should not be too concerned if your essay strays slightly from the topic or if you interpret the question creatively. While you will need to stay within the boundaries of the question or topic posed, you should remember that these boundaries are quite flexible.

For example, Harvard may ask, "Evaluate a significant experience or achievement that has special meaning to you" while Stanford may ask, "Tell us about a conversation you've had that changed your perspective or was otherwise meaningful to you." At first, these two questions seem to require two separate essays. Not true.

Say, for example, that you want to write about your father (which is the topic one of us used for the Harvard, Princeton, and Yale essays), and you plan to show how his making you breakfast every morning has helped to shape your outlook on life. While this essay would certainly answer the first question about a significant experience, it could also answer the second question if you started it with the following introduction:

Although I have had many great conversations with my father, one of the most meaningful was unspoken...

Thus, you could submit the essay that you wrote for Harvard about how your father's actions have influenced your life for Stanford's essay even though you are not writing specifically about a spoken "conversation." It is important, of course, to make sure you tell the reader in the introduction that you are interpreting the essay question in a less than literal way.

This is the essence of "recycling." Since the first essay for Harvard was so great (it took over a month to perfect) it only makes sense to try to use it as many times as possible.

Your essay on your father could also work for such topics as "Describe your saddest moment" if you began the essay by defining your saddest moment as the day you realized that you would soon be leaving home and would not be able to continue to spend every morning with your father. You could use your essay to answer a current events question by selecting the breakdown of the American family as the topic to lead into your own experience of having a strong, influential father figure.

In short, you should not think of each question from each school as requiring a totally original essay. While you will have to craft three or four well-written, concise, and thought-provoking essays, you will be able to use them with minor modifications for almost all of your applications.

When selecting the topics for your essays, keep in mind their potential for being recycled. We will go into much greater detail about the strategies for recycling in the next chapter. In the meantime, concentrate on writing your essays first, since the success of recycling requires you to have at least a few good essays.

The 5 Step Writing Workshop

It's time to get down to business with the actual writing. This workshop lays out everything you need to do from choosing a topic to doing the final spell check. Following the workshop are highly important *Essay-Writing Absolute Don'ts* as well as a list of *Totally Dumb Topics* you should read before you get started. Without further ado let's take a look at the first step.

STEP 1: Brainstorm Topics

Surprise! Here is a pop quiz for you. Is it better: a) to think of interesting topics regardless of the specific essay questions; or b) to read the questions and then think of only topics that directly address them. Answer: you need to do a little of both. (Trick question, huh?)

First, familiarize yourself with all of the essay questions that you need to answer. Read them over several times but don't limit your ideas yet.

While keeping the essay questions in the back of your mind, start jotting down all of the possible experiences, themes, and aspects of your life about which you could write. Remember that the object of brainstorming is to reach deep into the recesses of your mental filing cabinet and pull out the greatest number of potential essay topics possible.

The only rule for brainstorming is: Anything goes. Write down every idea that pops into your head, and do not eliminate anything. Even if some ideas lack the seed of a brilliant essay, they may lead you to think of others that do. The following questions should help you to get your list started:

▶ What are your favorite activities and hobbies? Why do you enjoy them?

▶ Do you have any special talents or skills?

▶ Who have been the most influential people in your life? The most memorable? The most interesting?

▶ What have you done during the past four summers?

▶ What was your best day/experience? Worst? Funniest?

▶ How have you changed in the past four years?

▶ What was the most memorable experience you have had with your parents? Brother or sister? Best friend? Teacher?

▶ What accomplishment are you proud of the most?

▶ What makes you special or unique?

▶ What is your strongest quality?

▶ What is a strong belief or philosophy that you hold?

As you answer these questions, allow your mind to wander to other questions. The point is to let your imagination go free and not to eliminate anything.

You should also enlist the help of parents and teachers in the brainstorming process because they may remember something that has slipped your mind.

When you run out of ideas, take a break and do something else. You will be surprised at how often ideas come when you least expect them. Be sure you carry a note pad around to record any serendipitous inspirations. By the end of a week or so, you should have a fairly comprehensive list of potential topics.

STEP 2: Narrow The List Of Possible Topics

Once you are pretty certain you have some potential winners on your list, you will need to start narrowing the field. The way to do this is to select topics that are important to you and which reflect your personality.

If the topic or the way in which you plan to approach the topic does not seem original, put a big fat "X" through it. The best way to insure that your topic or approach is original is to refer to the *Essay-Writing Absolute Don'ts* and *Totally Dumb Topics* sections in this chapter. Even if your idea seems good, if it is similar to any of the topics in our *Don'ts* list, you can count on 90% of your competition to write on the same "original" topic or in the same way.

Ask yourself these questions about your list of ideas:

▶ If your topic or subject is one that many applicants might write about (e.g., travel, parents, sports) do you have a unique approach that will insure that your essay will not sound like everyone else's?

▶ Does your idea have good supporting examples or stories? Your essay needs to have concrete details about things that you have done or experienced. Topics that allow you to elaborate on one or two of your activities or achievements are especially good.

▶ Can your idea be expressed within the limits of the essay? You should eliminate any topic that you know will require more than the given space to write. Topics that require 2,000 words to properly explain but that are summarized in 500 words often turn out sounding overly simplistic or are incredibly difficult to follow since many key points and explanations have to be omitted.

▶ Will your essay be interesting and creative? This is a very simple question but one that is hard to answer truthfully. Take a step back when answering this question and put yourself in the place of the admissions officer who has already read 300 or so essays and has just grabbed yours, which also happens to be the last before he or she can go home. Will your essay pique the interest of this tired admissions officer? Will the topic or your approach to the question make the admissions officer want to read past the introduction? Just because a topic is original does not always guarantee that it will be interesting. Use your best judgment by constantly asking if you would be interested in reading about your topic or experience.

▶ Can you present the topic in a way that will appeal to a wide audience? Do you have to have specific knowledge of the topic in order to understand it? For example, if your topic is a legal interpretation of the U.S. Tax Code or involves detailed scientific or technological terminology that can't be simplified, it may be better to choose something a little less complicated.

▶ Will the topic show the real you? Is it truly meaningful to you? Does your topic involve some insight into who you are, how you think, or what your passions are?

▶ Can the topic be recycled? If you write an essay on the topic, can you use the essay in several different applications?

Hopefully after paring down your list you will still have at least 10 to 15 ideas left. Prioritize these ideas according to their significance to you. Writing about something that you truly feel for will naturally transfer onto paper and will convey your feelings and passions to the admissions officers.

STEP 3: Razzle And Dazzle! Answer The Question Uniquely

Now that you know what you want to write about, write! You will find that some ideas that seemed promising do not translate very well to paper while others that were lower on your list end up making great essays. Unfortunately, the only way to tell if an idea will be a good essay is to try to write it.

Many of our ideas for college essays turned out to be too difficult to write in 500 words or appeared silly or just plain boring after we started writing. We often had to return to the brainstorming process. But after many false starts a few topics began to emerge as having real potential.

Before we leave you to your work, read a few of the writing tips that follow. It's a good idea to review them from time to time while you are writing. Also, read the *Essay-Writing Absolute Don'ts* and *Totally Dumb Topics* sections before you start writing.

Be Yourself. It is important to show the admissions officers the real you. You want to show why you think or act the way you do, what drives you, or what has moved you. As we said before, choose only the topics that are truly meaningful to you. Speak in your own voice. If you felt secretly happy that your evil opponent lost the quiz bowl, say so. By explaining how you really felt and not how you think the admissions committee would like for you to have felt, you will not only be truthful but will also help to insure that your essay is original.

Razzle, Dazzle, And Captivate Your Audience. When you begin writing, keep in mind that you need to write a truly memorable essay. You want your essay to razzle, dazzle, and captivate your audience. To do this, you need to draw the admissions officers into your essay with a quick, catchy, and creative introduction. You want to pique their curiosity by posing questions they will want the answers to and dilemmas they too have faced. Most important, you want the admissions officers to be able to relate to your essay (not necessarily to the actual events but to the feelings involved).

How you write is just as important as what you write. You should constantly ask yourself if you would be interested in your essay if you were the reader. Imagine yourself as the admissions officer as you read the first few paragraphs and ask yourself what makes you want to finish it? Do not just rely on your opinion. Seek the opinions of others. If your essay does not captivate, does not impel the reader to finish, you will need to rework it.

Create Some Mystery At The Forefront. Start your essay with an introduction that surprises the readers and makes them want to read past the first sentence. For example, you could start your essay with a description of your fear of the sounds of heavy artillery and roaring rapids when you are talking not about your latest trek to the firing range or your summer trip down the Colorado River but actually about your phobia of visiting the dentist. Keep in mind, however, that you have a limited space and therefore your introduction will have to be fairly brief. Do not get too carried away with your own creativity.

Raise Intriguing Questions Or Dilemmas. Ponder questions to which you think the admissions officers would be interested in finding the answers. If you raise a question or a dilemma you faced, ask yourself if the reader would be interested in knowing the results of your decision.

Use Original Language. Try to describe people, places, and events in a unique–but not awkward–style. Appeal to the different senses. What can the reader see from your essay? Hear? Smell? (Hopefully nothing rotten.) By adding rich detail you can often turn an ordinary topic into a one-of-a-kind masterpiece. The more you can bring the reader into your essay by using description the better. Try to think of language as a toy, and play with it. Just make sure that if you use unfamiliar words, you use them correctly. It is better to use ordinary language correctly than to use roller coaster-exciting language incorrectly.

Be Witty, But Only If You Can. Showing your sense of humor will help to make your essay memorable. If you can make the admissions officers laugh or giggle, it will be a definite plus for your application. But, do not go overboard with the humor and remember to have someone else check to make sure that what you think is funny really is funny. Admissions officers love essays that make them laugh. However, admissions officers also despise essays that intentionally try to be funny but are not or that use humor that is simply silly or immature. Our advice is to forget about trying to be funny and just tell an interesting story. If your story is well told and interesting, chances are that any inherent humor in it will show through.

By keeping these points in mind, you should be able to write a decent first draft. Remember that an original essay employs a unique angle, addresses a meaningful question or dilemma, and is crafted with thoughtful language.

STEP 4: Write For Perfection: Rewrite, Edit, Rewrite, And Edit Again, With Help From Editors

If you are like us, the first draft of your essay will be a rough skeleton at best. You will need to rewrite many times to tweak it to perfection. Throughout the editing process, keep in mind that your objectives are: 1) to reveal something about you; and 2) to razzle and dazzle the admissions officers.

Unfortunately, spending so much time looking at the same essay can cause temporary blindness to mistakes and lapses in the ability to differentiate between what you want to say and what your essay actually says. Your enthusiasm for reading with a critical eye may wane by the 15th rewrite, and what may make perfect sense to you because you know the story intimately may not make any sense to an outside reader.

There is an old but very true saying that behind every good writer there is an even better editor. Countless literary masterpieces would not be the great works that they are if it were not for the editors who made them so. To produce the best possible essay; you must, must, must find people to read it. Your editors, you will discover, will provide you with the most valuable information and suggestions on how to improve your work. Good editors include parents, teachers, counselors, siblings, and friends.

When you have found a couple of courageous volunteers to be editors, make sure that they know what to do. We have included a letter you can give to your editors to help them understand the purpose of the college essay and how to edit it correctly.

When your editors are finished, heed their advice. Do not take their criticisms personally since no matter how much it may hurt your feelings, their advice is going to improve your essays. Consider each of their suggestions, no matter how much you may disagree with them. Even if you think a section is crystal clear, if they are a little confused you'd better change it.

One final note about editors. It will be to your benefit to find at least two. While some tend to look at the big picture, the overall theme and message of your essay, others will focus on details like grammar, spelling, punctuation, and word usage. You want both of these types of editors to read your essays. So don't hold back on asking someone because of any reservations about sharing the personal feelings in your essays. This is one time when you cannot afford to let your fear of embarrassment get in the way of turning out a good essay.

Help Your Editors Learn How To Edit

College essays have a specific purpose—to convince the admissions officers that they should admit you. Your editors, while they may be excellent editors in every way, may not be familiar with this kind of writing or with how to persuade admissions officers that you are the greatest candidate of all time.

Thus, it is important to provide them with information about the purpose of the college essay and what you are trying to convey—*in writing.* Verbal instructions may be forgotten, but your editors cannot so easily ignore written instructions. The following article offers a short explanation that you can give to each of your editors.

How To Edit College Application Essays Masterfully

Most college admissions officers do not hesitate to admit that the essay is the single most important element in the admissions process. Because of this, students need to seek trustworthy editors to guide them in writing their essays and to offer them advice about how to make overall improvements. Since the college essay is a very specialized type of writing, the following tips are designed to help you masterfully edit these essays.

#1 The essay should focus on the student and reveal something about him or her. In a process that is oftentimes dominated by impersonal test scores and GPAs, most admissions officers view the essay as their only chance to get to know the student as an individual. Because of this expectation, you should make sure that the student offers some insight about who he or she is or about his or her way of thinking. This does not have to be done overtly, but when you are finished reading the essay, you should feel that you have a better understanding (as well as a mental picture) of the writer's personality.

#2 The essay should be creative and interesting. Admissions officers read stacks of essays each day. The ones that they remember, naturally, are those that are creative. Does the introduction draw you in? Is the essay unique or does it approach its topic in an unusual way? If not, you should identify where in the essay you lost interest. Does the essay start out strong but then lose its momentum? How can the essay be spiced up? How can the student take a different or more creative approach to the topic?

#3 The essay needs to be clear and flow smoothly with nice transitions. Are there any areas that you didn't understand? Is there a gap between what the author knows and what the reader actually understands? Are the transitions smooth and does the story make sense?

#4 The essay should make you like the student or want to meet him or her. Since you already know the student (and presumably like him or her), imagine this essay is your first introduction. Would you like to meet the author? Is the student portrayed in a likable, interesting way? Would he or she be a valuable addition to your school?

#5 The essay should be flawless. Content isn't all that counts. Check the student's spelling, grammar, and word usage as well. Any mistakes you find are ones that the admissions officers won't.

#6 Be honest. The most important thing you can do is to give your honest evaluation of the student's essay. If you think that the piece needs improvement, don't be afraid to tell the student. Offer as much constructive criticism as possible and suggestions for improvement.

We hope that these tips will help you to better evaluate the college essay. Just by taking the time to read it, however, you are making a valuable contribution towards helping the student get into college.

Step 5: Last Nit-Picky Points Before Submitting Your Essay

Perfect Your Spelling And Grammar. With so much riding on your essays, you don't want something as simple as a spelling or grammar mistake to count against you.

Unfortunately, relying on your computer's spell checker is not enough. You need to spend the extra time to personally scrutinize your work. (This does not mean giving it the once over at two o'clock in the morning!)

Don't think we're crazy, but one trick you might want to try is to read your essay backwards. Since your essay will be totally incomprehensible, it will force you to focus only on the words and their spelling. Also, if you are unsure of how to use a word, make sure you look it up in a dictionary.

The best way to perfect your spelling and grammar is to have as many knowledgeable editors as possible read your essay. They will often catch what you will miss.

Count Your Words. This is another one of those little things that you do not want to count against you (no pun intended). When the application asks for a 500 word essay, you can go over by 75 or 100 words; but trying to slip in 2 or 3 extra pages will not be acceptable. Limits are set to insure that everyone has a fair chance since it would be unfair to compare a 1,000 word essay to a 400 word essay. Plus, logistically, admission officers would never be able to finish their job if everybody exceeded the guidelines.

For more tips on how to lighten an overweight essay, refer to *How To Shorten A Long Essay* at the end of the Chapter 6.

The Essay-Writing Absolute Don'ts

Perhaps as important as knowing what to do is knowing what *not* to do. With this knowledge, you will be able to avoid what we call the "90% Trap." You may think that writing about the jubilation you felt after you scored the winning touchdown is an original and inspiring essay bound to be your free ticket into a highly competitive college. But unless the college is recruiting you for your athletic ability, you will be sorely disappointed.

Believe it or not, 90% of college applicants will write identical essays. They may not write about the exact same topic, like football, but they will deal with similar topics and themes (e.g., "winning isn't everything," "we should learn to appreciate other cultures," etc.) Many of these essays will answer the stated questions in predictable ways and in nearly identical styles or tones.

Imagine that you are a college admissions officer at Harvard. Each year your office receives anywhere from 15,000 to 20,000 applications. If you have to read several hundred application essays and 90% of them echo the themes of those you have already read, which applications will stand out when it comes time to narrow the pool? Of course, it will be those with unique and original essays. As an applicant, it is imperative that you are among this top 10% and avoid the common essay traps that snare the others.

The following is a description of the most common mistakes that applicants make in their essays. Do not be surprised if some of the ideas you have for your essay show up on this list. Trust us, they are on 90% of other applicants' lists as well. Your advantage is that you will be able to recognize and avoid these potential disasters before you start to write.

DON'T Try To Be Someone Else. The most important thing to remember when writing your essay is to *be yourself.* This means you should avoid portraying yourself as Mother Teresa when the closest you have ventured to philanthropy was watching 10 minutes of the Muscular Dystrophy telethon.

Often applicants are tempted to create an alter-ego of what they think is the perfect student. Because the essay is a creative effort, it is very easy to stretch the truth and exaggerate feelings and opinions. One admissions officer at a small private school in the South was notorious for his critique of some essays in which he used a rubber stamp engraved with a pair of horns and the word "bull."

How can admissions officers tell a fake or forced essay? Easy. Phony essays don't match the other areas of the student's application and they often tend to be overwritten and melodramatic. These essays also lack details that can only come from real experiences.

Admissions officers have read thousands of essays, and if they believe your essay to be less than the truth, you will ruin not only your reputation but also any chances of getting in. Besides, we guarantee that there is something about you that has the makings of a stellar essay. If you spend the time developing this in your essay, you will be able to blow the admissions officers off their feet in a way that no pretense or exaggeration could.

DON'T Write About Common Experiences Commonly. This is one of the most predominant and dangerous mistakes applicants make. To avoid it, you must resist the temptation to write about an ordinary experience in an ordinary way.

Ideally, you will be able to come up with both original topics and original ways to write about them. However, since the essay questions tend to limit what you can write about, you need to be most concerned with how you are going to approach your topic. For example, tens of thousands of students will write about: a) how being class president, club founder, or team captain was their greatest achievement; b) how their mother, father, or teacher has been the most influential person in their lives; or c) how they were the key person in winning the "big" game, match, or academic decathlon.

It is fine for you to write about an *ordinary* topic. The key is that you write your essay in an *extraordinary* fashion. Ask yourself: Are you presenting the material in a way that is unique to you, in a way that no one else can? What slant are you going to give to the topic or question to make your essay unusual and unique?

DON'T Flex. For some strange reason, many applicants have a tendency to write about the great mysteries of the world or momentous philosophical debates in an effort to show admissions officers their intelligence and sophistication. At Harvard we called people who wrote essays which aimed to impress rather than educate "flexors," as in people who flex their intellectual muscles.

While these essays attempt to present the illusion of sophistication, they are usually entirely without substance. Often they simply parrot back the opinions of others in a slightly different form, and unless the writer is indeed an expert on the subject, such essays are completely unoriginal.

College admissions officers do not want to read some 18-year-old's diatribe on the nature of truth or the validity of Marxism. And admissions officers most certainly do not want to be lectured. Essays that try to impress with pseudo-intellectualism are definite candidates for the trash bin. Remember the goal of the essay. Admissions officers want to learn about the kind of person you are and the things that you have done.

not again [handwritten note in left margin]

However, if your passion is indeed sociological theory or reading Marx is your beloved pastime, then by all means write about it, but put it in perspective. Write about how you became interested in Marx rather than outlining your interpretation of Marxist theory.

DON'T Write In Clichés. Clichés include phrases like "all is well that ends well," "practice what you preach," and "don't cry over spilled milk." To you, phrases like these may seem clever. You may even use them regularly. But to admissions officers, clichés are not only trite but they also reveal a lack of sophistication and originality. If you use clichés you will sound no better than a well-trained parrot. You want the admissions committee to know that you are a capable writer who has the imagination and skill to write without the crutch of other people's overused phrases.

DON'T Over Quote. Along a similar vein as clichés, quotations also tend to make essays sound parrot like. In analytical essays, quotations are often a valuable component. However, in the limited space of the college essay you need to maintain your originality and not allow too many quotations to distract from your voice.

Since quotations are not your own words, never use them in a critical point or in place of your own analysis. Using a very well-known quotation is especially dangerous since 90% of the other applicants (who have not spent the time to prepare by reading this book) will almost certainly use similar quotations in their essays. If you want your essay to be memorable, it must be kept original. Now is the time to put aside the *Bartlett's Book of Quotations* and start writing for yourself.

DON'T Cross The Line Between Creativity And Absurdity. Most of the time the problem with college essays is that they are not creative enough. However, some applicants, in an effort to insure that their essay is one-of-a-kind, go too far on the creative side. Rather than sounding original and insightful, the essay appears trite and silly. A general rule is that you want your work to be as creative as possible but not so creative that admissions officers won't take it seriously.

If you have a question about whether your work crosses the line in the creativity department, you'd better get a second or third

Synopsis Of Temporary Insanity In An Essay

The following summary is a true instance of creativity gone overboard. The most frightening thing about this example is that at the time it was written, the student truly felt that he had created an intellectual masterpiece and never dreamed that it might seem remotely silly or outrageous.—Jim Good

The author, a high school friend, wrote his essay as if he had been reborn as a cockroach. While the premise is not a bad one, the way in which it was executed was disastrous. It began with him—the cockroach—crawling out of a toilet bowl. The toilet was not your ordinary commode either, but was also a meta-phor for school where he felt he had just been running around in circles without making any forward progress. So having finally discovered a way out of the john, he crawled around his new environment discovering all kinds of wonderful things.

Ok, already this essay was a little weird since it was written in the first person of an insect. At this point the admissions officer was probably wondering if my friend was just trying to be extremely creative. Unfortunately as the story progressed it turned out that while the narrative was no doubt creative it had crossed the line into the territory of the absurd.

I'll just highlight a few of the adventures on which my friend as cockroach em-barked. There was his encounter with the toaster where he ate some bread crumbs and pondered what a rich land—as evidenced by the sourdough and pumpernickel crumbs—he had discovered. There was the nearly fatal encoun-ter with the roach motel. It was a good thing my friend did not decide to get a room. And towards the end was a climactic battle between good and evil where he defended his right to life and liberty when threatened by a hysterical insec-ticide-wielding housewife.

I have to admit that my friend's essay was very creative and would probably have gotten an "A" in a creative writing class. But a college admissions essay it was not. It seems that to more than a few college admissions officers this essay was just too much. While acknowledging his creativity, they could not take it seriously and probably questioned his judgment in submitting such an inappropriate essay. The college essay is not a place to debut experimental writing. My friend did not get accepted at any of his top choice schools, but (I am happy to report) he did graduate top in his class from a smaller private college. His major was, as you may have guessed, creative writing.

opinion. If one of your readers feels that the essay may be a little too off-the-wall, then you need to tone it down or even abandon it. The college application is not the place to experiment and take radical chances. While you should write creatively, beware of the easy crossover into silliness.

DON'T Go Thesaurus Wild. Using creative wording is one of the most definite "Dos" of writing your essay. However, writing your essay in the words of your thesaurus is one of the worst mistakes you can make.

First, some of the alternate words you find in a thesaurus will probably be unfamiliar to you. This means that if you use these alternate words, you run a high likelihood of using them awkwardly or incorrectly.

Second, admissions officers possess a keen radar for picking out essays coauthored by a thesaurus. Call the admissions officers psychic for their ability to pick out the thesaurus-aided essays, but they really are not that hard to find. Here, for example, is an excerpt from an essay that was definitely under the influence of the thesaurus:

To recapitulate myself, I am an aesthetic and erudition-seeking personage. My superlative design in effervescence is to prospect divergent areas of the orb and to conceive these divergent cultures through the rumination of the lives of indisputable people.

This essay is the worst of its kind. The author is clearly trying to be a "flexor," but has totally butchered correct word usage, not to mention common sense.

DON'T Write A Humorous Essay If You Are Not Humorous. Very few people can write truly humorous essays although thousands will try. Even if it may seem funny to you, all it takes is for one admissions officer to feel the opposite and you can kiss that letter of acceptance good-bye.

Unless you are a truly gifted humor writer, the test being that people other than yourself have said so, then stay away from the humorous essays. If you do insist on writing a humorous essay then be very certain that it is not of the silly variety. Admissions officers hate nothing more than feeling that you are not taking the application seriously.

Of course, using small doses of humor within a serious essay is desirable, but if you are not used to using humor then make sure to confirm the existence of real humor in your work with editors.

DON'T Resort To Gimmicks. Previous applicants have written their essays in fluorescent highlighter or nail polish, sent cookies baked in the shape of the university's seal along with the essay, and enclosed audio "mood" music that admissions officers were supposed to play while reading their essays to create the right "ambiance." These tricks, while entertaining, are no substitute for actual substance.

While printing your essay in any other color than black is simply a bad idea from the point of view of readability, sending videos, audio tapes, computer programs, and other multimedia is also usually a poor idea since they are often less impressive to admissions officers than applicants may think.

The exception to this rule is when your work is truly outstanding (this having been verified by someone other than yourself). If you have filmed a documentary that won honors at the Cannes festival or recorded a platinum selling album, then by all means include it. But think twice about submitting an audio tape of your amateur band, *Blood, Depression, and Withdrawal,* that congregates in your garage every other month or so.

Totally Dumb Topics To Avoid

A few words should be said about plain old dumb topics. As a rule, don't choose dumb topics. What are these topics that are off limits no matter how interesting, humorous, or scintillating their related tales may be? Many of these are obvious, but you would be surprised at how many students simply lose their sense of judgment when writing their essays. The only exception to this list is if you can "undumb" them by writing about them in an intelligent way. But unless you can do this well (and have your work checked by several editors) it is much safer simply to stay away from these subjects. These taboo topics include:

Sex. Answering a question about the most momentous event of her life, one student wrote about, shall we say, a very private experience. We're sure this student's essay provided something to gossip about in the college admissions office, but it certainly was not an appropriate topic.

Sex may sell in any other media, but not for college admissions. It is okay to write about your experience as a sexual abuse counselor or your volunteer work to prevent premarital sex as long as your focus is on the work that you do and not the explicit experiences of your clients.

You should never write about your or others' sexual experience, methods of birth control, prostitution, turn-ons, etc. We do not think we need to detail what would happen if such an essay fell onto the desk of a conservative admissions officer from a Puritan East Coast school.

Crimes, Misdemeanors, And School Violations You Have Committed. On your application, you are required to report any serious criminal activity, suspensions, or disciplinary problems. This is the one area of the application that you want to be able to leave blank. But if you are not able to, your essay is certainly not the place to highlight any trouble with the law or lack of judgment that you had as an adolescent.

While the story may be interesting and although you may think your candor will impress the admissions officers, what you will actually be doing is setting off warning signals. No school wants gang members, graffiti artists, or thieves.

Even if you have learned your lesson and wish to write about your rehabilitation, imagine what would happen if one of the admissions officers has been a victim of crime or believes that rehabilitation is impossible or simply does not want to risk admitting someone who has a tendency to not follow rules.

One student we know did not follow this advice and thought that his tale of setting 200 live rats loose in his school's hallways would show the admissions officers his creative side. The admissions officers clearly didn't see the value of this type of creativity and he was rejected from nearly every school to which he applied.

Drunkenness Or Getting High. One student thought it would be particularly entertaining to describe how he thought he was a chicken during his last substance-induced high. It may have been entertaining, but it did not gain him admission. No matter how humorous or memorable your alcohol or drug-induced antics may be, they are not appropriate for your essay. Like tales of criminal acts, they may make the admissions officers think you need professional help before higher education.

Your Bad Grades. Some guides to the admissions process suggest that you write explanations for a less than perfect academic record. We strongly advise against this because it not only emphasizes that your grades have not been stellar, but it also makes you sound as if you do not take responsibility for your actions and that you tend to look for excuses when bad things happen.

Instead of trying to explain away bad grades, focus instead on what kept you busy or what kept you motivated. Such an essay will very likely convince the committee to overlook your lack of academic performance in favor of your other talents and virtues. Admissions officers know that not everyone can get straight "A's." If grades are not your strong point then you need to show them what is.

A sad but amusing story is of a student who spent his entire essay explaining why he did not receive perfect grades. His reason was that he thought that he had a brain tumor, and throughout the semester he was so consumed by his stress over this potential disease that he could not do his homework. At the end of his semester, he finally went to a doctor who confirmed that he did not, after all, have a brain tumor. Unfortunately, however, his explanation for his bad grades did not help him get into college, although we are sure that the admissions officers were nonetheless entertained by his hypochondria.

Description Of Why X University Is Perfect. The admissions officers are already familiar with the beautiful architecture, rigorous academic courses, and opportunities to meet extraordinary people at their universities. So you would only be wasting valuable space informing them of things they already know, especially since they probably know more about the college than you do. An exception is if you have a creative way of approaching this. This means that you do more than regurgitate the information in the glossy brochures or pile on meaningless platitudes.

The Dysfunction Of Your Family. It may be true that your family has been the most influential group of people in your life and that through your family's difficulties you have learned a lot about life. However, you should never criticize your family's dysfunctions too harshly. Do not complain about how you never felt that your mother loved you, how your father is essentially nonexistent, or about how screwed up your youngest sister is.

Such essays raise questions about your mental stability and your ability to deal with hardships maturely. Furthermore, nobody likes a complainer. If your father was not around much while you were growing up, then focus on how this helped you to become independent rather than how it scarred you for life. Writing about family difficulties is not taboo, but make sure you show the positive things that you have learned and how you have overcome such hardships. If you cannot in all honesty find something good about your family then simply do not write an essay about them.

Death. Your goal is certainly not to depress the admissions officers. While death is a powerful topic, if they finish your essay feeling totally gloomy, they may very easily assume that such gloominess is a reflection of your personality. After all, as the author you have the power to evoke certain feelings from the reader and what you choose to make them feel also says a lot about you. This does not mean that you cannot write about memories of people who have passed away. Just do not fall into the trap of dwelling on death itself, which could make for a powerful, but thoroughly depressing, essay.

Your Mental Imbalances Or Insecurities. The last thing that admissions officers want to read is your self-evaluation of the mental imbalances or insecurities that you have. Surprisingly, some students use the essay as their forum for revealing their deepest insecurities. Some even rationalize that being totally honest about their shortcomings is the best way to write a genuine essay.

One student focused on her belief that the world, including the admissions officers, were conspiring to her downfall. She wrote that the only way she would believe otherwise was if she were accepted by the college. It appears that there must have been some sort of conspiracy after all since she was not accepted!

While this strategy of revealing your insecurities may indeed show the admissions officers who "you" really are, this is not the "you" that you want revealed. Describing such personal issues as how you have always felt unsure about whether you will ever amount to anything in the future, how you always view yourself as an underachiever, or how you are frequently depressed will signal to the admissions officers that you may not be ready to handle the pressures of college.

Your Plan To Bring Peace And Harmony To The World Or Any Other Unrealistic Dream. It is true that admissions officers like young people with bright ideas and determination. But when you write a whole essay about your plan to bring about world peace, stop hunger, or end poverty, you sound more like a competitor in the Miss America Pageant than an intelligent high school student with a firm grasp of reality. There is nothing wrong with having ideals and dreams, just do not spend a whole essay writing about them. An essay about your dreams of doing the impossible, unless you can back it up with concrete examples of what you have done, will only make you sound unrealistic and naive.

Furthermore, such essays give nothing substantial to the admissions committee. Anybody can say they want to end world hunger. More than a few applicants will fall into this trap and will write at great lengths about what they want to do in the future when in fact what they should be writing about is what they have already done. Resist any temptation to impress the admissions officers with your grand plans since you will end up sounding more deserving of a rhinestone-studded tiara than a mortarboard.

The Big Game. Thousands will write about the Big Game, the Big Match, or the Big Tournament. Be careful with this kind of topic since it is so common. If you write about some "Big Game," be sure that you have an approach that will be different from the rest. Ask yourself when writing if others could have had the same experience and might also write about it in a similar way. This essay requires a lot of thought to be successful. But if you do have a creative approach in mind then by all means write about the "Big Game."

Specific Tips For Specific Questions

Besides the main 500-word essay question, colleges may also ask you other more specific questions. Often these questions are shorter, but this does not mean they are less difficult. Since the admissions officers are reviewing your entire application, you don't want to skimp on these essays.

In this section, we will give you some tips for answering the most common specific questions. All of the same rules apply to these shorter questions as to the major essay questions. You should always razzle and dazzle your audience with creativity and honesty, rewrite and edit continuously, and seek the help of editors.

However, because of the more narrow topic guidelines, there are techniques that apply specifically to these essays. The most important thing to keep in mind is that there are no wrong answers to these questions.

The reality is that the admissions officers are *not* very interested in what your answer really is. They don't care what subject in school or which book you like best. But they do care about what your attraction to organic chemistry or Tolstoy says about you. Throughout all of your essays, keep in mind that your primary goal is to tell the admissions officers about you, your thoughts and opinions, and your growth. Secondary is your actual answer to the question.

Here are some examples of more specific questions from recent applications and some tips on answering them:

Your Favorite Book

Don't write a book report. No matter how interesting it may be, the admissions officers are not interested in the plot, characters, or literary analysis of your favorite book.

Instead, write about how your favorite book relates to you. Write about how you have applied the lessons from the work in your daily life, detail why it is your favorite, or explain how it has affected you personally. Through this essay, the admissions officers want to learn less about the actual book–they can browse through it at a bookstore any time–and more about you.

Being Or Meeting A Historical Or Other Person And Describing The Most Influential Person In Your Life

Don't write a biography. The last thing that the admissions officers want to read is a biography of Susan B. Anthony or Martin Luther King, Jr. While the stories of well-known personalities are often interesting, the admissions officers could just as easily have glanced through an encyclopedia. Don't waste your space.

About half the students will select their mother or father as the most influential person in their life. Unless you are sure that you can describe the role of a parent in a way that will be unlike other students' essays, try to choose someone else. The same goes for the President of the United States, Bill Gates, or any other popular figure. If you can write about these people in a creative way, do so. If you can't, pick someone whom your competitors won't.

Explain why you choose who you choose. Make your reasons for your decision clear to the admissions officers. Explain why you think this person's contributions are important. Describe how what they have done has affected your life, how it has motivated you, or how you think it will inspire others. Concentrate most on how the person has made an impact on your life. After all, this essay is about you, not about the person you choose.

Your Academic Or Intellectual Interests

Admissions officers don't want to hear *what* you know about Eastern philosophy; they want to know *why* you have dedicated a shrine in your room to Confucius. They want to find out *why* you are interested in certain academic or intellectual areas. Who introduced you to it? Why are you intrigued? Do you plan to pursue your interest? Tell them how your interest relates to or says something about you, not about the interest itself.

Your Ideal Future Roommate

Describing the person with whom you will fight over the telephone, complain to about spending too much time in the bathroom, and sleep three feet above in a bunk bed leaves some room for creativity. Use this opportunity to show your imagination.

Just make sure to focus on saying something about yourself while at the same time describing your ideal roommate. Explain why you would like your roommate to enjoy late night TV or why you hope that he or she has a pet goldfish named Ned. Use the description of your ideal roommate to show what qualities you admire in a person.

Your Greatest Achievement

When colleges ask this question, the truth is that they are not solely interested in what it is that you have accomplished. Rather, colleges ask this question because they want to know how you view your own accomplishments and what has motivated you to do the things that you have.

Don't just give facts and statistics. It is not enough for you to merely describe what you have done. Admissions officers are not interested in reading an expanded form of your resume. All of this stuff appears in your application form anyway.

They will be interested, however, in what your description of your accomplishment says about you. They want to know why you think it was your most outstanding achievement, what standard you measure it by, what your motivations were, and how you felt. They want to understand not only *what* you did but *why* you did it. They also want to know how your accomplishment has affected your life and how it has changed your perspectives.

Ask yourself what your answer says about you since this is the question admissions officers will be asking themselves. Finally, since we're talking about a presumably significant achievement that you are proud of, be careful of going overboard on the bragging. You want to be honest but you also want to keep some humility, and you certainly want to avoid appearing arrogant.

Hobbies

Don't just describe your hobby. Don't merely write what your hobby is or how long you've done it. This tells the admissions officers nothing about you. They will be more interested in why you find enjoyment in creating knitted Barbie doll dresses than in actually how to knit.

Try to show yourself through your hobby. Explain why you have a passion for your hobby, what inspired you to begin it, or what it has taught you. If you have excelled at your hobby, by all means, now is the time to brag subtly.

A Page Of Your Autobiography

Lucky you. Chances are that you can easily recycle one of your essays for this question. Because of the open-endedness of this question, almost anything you have written is suitable. You can describe your favorite hobby, your greatest accomplishment, your family, or anything else of significance in your life because all of these topics would be a page in your autobiography.

The key thing is to make sure that you know how to recycle this material. You don't want to make it obvious that you are using an essay that you wrote to answer a different question. To learn more about how to recycle your essays, see Chapter 6. The only other thing to keep in mind is that like every other essay that you write, your goal is to tell the admissions officers something important about you.

Your Future Career Plans

Colleges may ask you about your future career plans in order to get a better idea of where you see yourself headed. Here again, colleges aren't interested in how final your decision is or exactly what you see yourself doing. Rather, they want to know what is motivating you to choose this career path. And don't worry, they won't hold you to your answer.

Don't write a job description. Unless the job you wish to have is so uncommon that the admissions officers will not know what it is, which is highly unlikely, don't simply provide a description of your future career. You also need not mention how much money you want to earn. Even if you are absolutely positive that your future career will result in your becoming the first 20-year-old self-made gazillionaire, don't share your financial dreams with the admissions officers. You don't want to present yourself as a greedy, dollar-track-minded individual, even if that's what you really are.

Learn The Magic Of Recycling And Check Out Examples Of The Good, Bad, And Ugly

Before you put this book aside and start your own essays, familiarize yourself with the art of recycling in Chapter 6 and read the example essays in Chapter 7. The *Recycling* chapter will save you time and your sanity if you are applying to many schools. Our strategies and tips as well as the *Essay-Writing Absolute Don'ts* can been seen in action in the real essays in Chapter 7. Happy writing!

THE MAGIC OF RECYCLING ESSAYS

In This Chapter
- ▲ How To Answer Any Question With Only One Essay
- ▲ Learn To Interpret The Questions To Fit Your Essay
- ▲ See Recycling In Action
- ▲ How To Make A Long Essay Short Or A Short Essay Long
- ▲ Important Checks When Recycling

Presto-Chango! Turn One Essay Into Many

Writing one essay can take weeks or even months. What if you plan to apply to 5, 10 or more colleges? Yikes! Does this mean you will have to skip school just so you have enough time to write 10 or more perfectly crafted and individual essays? Thankfully, despite how tempting playing hooky can be, the answer is "no."

Why go through the difficult and time-consuming essay-writing process again and again to answer each school's essay questions when you can modify a few essays to answer all of them? In fact, if you write three or four good essays, you will have enough to apply to an almost unlimited number of schools. Sound too good to be true? What makes this possible is the magical technique called "recycling."

In this chapter you will learn some of the finer techniques of recycling and see how to change a single essay so that it answers a variety of seemingly unrelated questions. Recycling does require some effort to pull off successfully. But we promise that after reading this chapter you will have the skills necessary to shed weeks off the essay writing process.

The Common Application: The Easiest Way To Recycle

The ultimate in recycling is to mail the exact same essay word for word to all of the colleges to which you are applying. While a fantasy for past applicants, this is increasingly becoming a reality through the growing acceptance of the Common Application.

The Common Application is a single application that various schools (including Harvard) accept in place of their own application. This means that if you are applying to more than one school that accepts the Common Application, you can send this application, virtually unchanged, to all of these schools.

But for those schools that do not accept the Common Application, which unfortunately is still the majority, you will need to learn the art of recycling.

How To Answer Any Question With Only One Essay

There are two secrets you need to know to understand how recycling works:

Secret #1: You don't have to answer the question the college asks, *at least not directly.*

Secret #2: The major changes necessary for most recycled essays are some modifications to the essay's introduction and conclusion. Obviously, a computer or word processor is highly recommended–if not essential–for this type of editing.

As we mentioned in the last chapter, the particular essay questions posed by the colleges are not important in and of themselves. Think of them as suggested topics that help you to focus your essays. What the admissions officers are really looking for is not what your actual answers are but an essay that contains your thoughts and opinions to help them gauge what kind of person you are and to show them your writing skills.

Therefore, while you do need to stay within the bounds of the question, the boundaries themselves are quite flexible.

Let's look at an example of how this might work. One year Harvard asked, "Evaluate a significant experience or achievement that has special meaning to you in 250 to 500 words." Since you are a smart applicant who has read this book, you would of course follow all of the tips in the last chapter and after several weeks have a perfect essay describing, for example, a hike in the Grand Canyon that changed your outlook on life. This essay directly addresses the Harvard question and could be mailed to them as is.

However, if you were also applying to Stanford you might think you need to write an entirely new essay to answer their question, "Describe a book, class, project, or person that you find intellectually exciting and explain why."

Before you begin brainstorming, wait a minute. If you have read any books along the lines of *Robinson Crusoe*, *Tom Sawyer*, *Huckleberry Finn*, or *The Heart of Darkness*, you could in your introduction begin by referring to one of these books, describing the importance of nature and adventure in the book and then showing how these same themes have affected your life.

Through the use of a good transition you could then attach word for word the main body of your Harvard essay describing your own adventure in the Grand Canyon and how it changed your views on life. In the conclusion you could again juxtapose your adventure with that of one of the characters or themes in the novel and reemphasize the significance of both the book and adventure in your life.

The result would be another perfect essay that only took a fraction of the time to write. The major requirement for recycling to be successful is that you have at least one good essay with which to begin. Remember that as powerful as recycling is, it will not improve a bad essay. In fact, a bad essay recycled and sent to 100 schools will still only yield 100 rejections.

Recycling In Action: A Case Study

Now that you have some sense of the usefulness of recycling, let's turn to a real example. In this case Anita, known as the "Queen of Recycling," was able to answer six different questions using only one essay. Anita's original essay was about how other people's prejudices about her have made her stronger. The power of her essay lies in her gripping introduction and in her mature confrontation with a difficult problem in this country today.

The original question Anita answered was for Columbia, "Write an essay which conveys to the reader a sense of who you are." This is a very common question, and Anita was able to send the same essay to several schools with almost no changes. However, some of the schools that Anita applied to asked more specific questions. With some thoughtful editing, however, Anita was able to modify her original essay to answer all of the following questions:

#1 Tell us about a conversation you've had that changed your perspective or was otherwise meaningful to you. (Stanford)

#2 Of all of the things you hope or expect to gain from your college experience (other than a degree!), which two or three would you place at the top of your list if you had to make up such a list today? (Princeton)

#3 Indicate a person who has had a significant influence on you, and describe that influence. (Common Application)

#4 Discuss some issue of personal, local, national or international concern and its importance to you. (Harvard)

#5 Pomona College defines diversity in broad terms including academic interests, ethnic background, educational opportunities, political views, socioeconomic environment, and personal pursuits among others. Reflect upon ways which you expect Pomona's diverse student body will affect your experiences inside and outside the classroom. (Pomona College)

The following is Anita's original essay, which answers Columbia's very broad question, "Write an essay which conveys to the reader a sense of who you are." After the original essay are examples of some of the major changes Anita made when she used the same essay to answer the other questions. You will see that by just adding a few sentences to the introduction or conclusion she was able to shift the focus of the essay to address the specific question posed while leaving the bulk of the essay untouched, the essence of recycling.

"Yo Soy" (Original Essay)

I am a Latina, but don't hold it against me. Please don't equate my last name, Rodriguez, with low intelligence or motivation. Don't look at my brown eyes and see an illegal immigrant who refuses to speak English preferring incomprehensible Español instead. Don't view my dark skin and black hair as exotic. Don't stereotype me as a Latin lover. Please don't judge me so readily. Others have done so too many times already.

On the first day of kindergarten my mother drove me to school. Before letting me out of the front seat of our old station wagon, she pulled me close, clasping her hands around my face for emphasis. "Take care of yourself," she said with a face so expressionless that I knew she meant it. As my feet hit the ground I heard her say, "You are a Latina. Be proud." At the time I didn't know what she meant but for some reason it stuck in my memory.

It was only as I grew older that I came to understand the meaning of her words. Throughout my education, I have been a minority at my schools. Instead of attending the schools in my neighborhood where 95 percent of the children are Latino, my mother arranged for me to be transferred to schools where 95 percent of the children are white, telling me I would receive a better education that way. At first, as with all innocent children, I did not notice any differences between my classmates and me. The first time I realized a difference, it was pointed out to me.

In the 6th grade we had a dance. My four girl friends and I lined up against one wall while the boys were against the opposite. After our teacher realized that the lines would remain that way all afternoon unless he did something, he guided five hesitant boys to our side of the room. Each of them chose one of my four friends to dance with, but the last boy, Bobby, did not choose me.

"Mr. Henshaw, I don't want to dance with a Mexican," he said, pulling back toward our teacher. Mr. Henshaw pulled Bobby to the side, and I could tell that he was scolding him. When he was finished, Bobby came up to me again and sullenly asked me to dance.

Although I had noticed that my hair did not fall down straight like the blonde and brunette hair of the other girls and that when we studied skin coloring in health class mine was darker than the rest, Bobby was the first to actually show me how being a Latina was different from being white.

Unfortunately, he was the first of many to remind me that I could be looked down on for who I was. Since the sixth grade dance, I have been told to return to Mexico, to stop stealing money through the welfare system, and to speak America's language. I was even threatened with having my Green Card revoked even through I don't have one, having been born here.

In spite of these bad experiences, I have been fortunate enough to rise through the education system to where I am now at a well-known high school which has a reputation for sending a large number of students to Ivy League colleges. The atmosphere at my high school often enforces the idea that we must compete for the limited number of positions at each top-ranked college. I have tried to stay out of this competition, but have become involuntarily involved.

Other students frequently mention to me, "Anita, you have it made. You're going to get into the college of your choice. What I wouldn't do to have the advantage of being Mexican, too." Or, "Anita, you are so lucky. Affirmative action really makes this whole college admissions process a piece of cake for you, doesn't it?"

At first the questions and comments of my fellow students really crushed, frustrated, and angered me. I wondered, do these students think that I should be flattered by their comments? Do they think that it is so easy to be a Latina and that I have not worked hard to achieve everything that I have? Would they really elect to be a Latina if they had the choice? If America's supposed best students in pursuit of higher education hold such beliefs, what hope was there at all for me?

As my fellow students continued to make such thoughtless comments, I came to realize that some of the people in this world would always judge me more by my last name than by my abilities, more by the hue of my skin than by my personality. It would be wonderful of course to live in a world where race didn't make a difference, but the sad fact is that such a world does not yet exist.

Although it has been difficult, I have come to face those who doubt me without getting angry. I have accepted that I will have to live and work with them and that they will continue to make assumptions about me. But, the difference now is that I have decided to fight against their cruel assumptions, not by feeling belittled, but by proving them wrong.

Today I do more than complain about the misguided attitudes that people have. I show them to be in err. Through my achievements and work I challenge anyone who has doubts about my abilities. I will continue to work hard to achieve the good grades and accomplishments that I already have. I finally know what my mother meant in the front seat of our station wagon. If other people choose to stereotype me, so be it. It won't change anything for me. I am a Latina and I am proud of who I am. *Yo soy latina.*

Changes To Introduction For Stanford's Question: "Tell us about a conversation you've had that changed your perspective or was otherwise meaningful to you." *Changes are noted in italics.*

(2nd Paragraph) On the first day of kindergarten my mother drove me to school. Before letting me out of the front seat of our old station wagon, she pulled me close, clasping her hands around my face for emphasis. "Take care of yourself," she said with a face so expressionless that I knew she meant it. As my feet hit the ground I heard her say, "You are a Latina. Be proud." *Although I didn't know it at the time, those simple words, that one-way conversation with my mother, would remain forever etched in my mind. At the time I had no idea what the significance of that conversation would be. But through the twelve years that it has taken me to learn the meaning of that exchange, it has always remained, perhaps subconsciously, the foundation of a strength which has helped me to deal with one of the greatest sources of frustration in my life.*

Changes To Conclusion For Princeton's Question: "Of all of the things you hope or expect to gain from your college experience (other than a degree!), which two or three would you place at the top of your list if you had to make up such a list today?" *Changes are noted in italics.*

(Last Paragraph) Today I do more than complain about the misguided attitudes that people have. I show them to be in err. Through my achievements and work I challenge anyone who has doubts about my abilities. *What I truly hope to gain from a Princeton educa-*

tion is the chance to acquire the skills and experience to continue to do this. I want to continue to work hard by challenging myself with the best education possible. I finally know what my mother meant in the front seat of our station wagon. If other people choose to stereotype me, so be it. It won't change anything for me. I am a Latina and I am proud of who I am. Yo soy latina.

Changes To Introduction For The Common Application's Question: "Indicate a person who has had a significant influence on you, and describe that influence." *Changes are noted in italics.*

(2nd Paragraph)   On the first day of kindergarten my mother drove me to school. Before letting me out of the front seat of our old station wagon, she pulled me close, clasping her hands around my face for emphasis. "Take care of yourself," she said with a face so expressionless that I knew she meant it. As my feet hit the ground I heard her say, "You are a Latina. Be proud." *Although I didn't know it at the time, those simple words from my mother would remain forever etched in my mind. At the time I had no idea how significant this moment would be. But in the twelve years that it has taken me to discover what my mother meant on that morning so many years ago, I believe that her words have helped me to come to terms with what has been a constant source of frustration in my life.*

Changes To Introduction For Harvard's Question: "Discuss some issue of personal, local, national or international concern and its importance to you." *Changes are noted in italics.*

(First Paragraph)   I am a Latina, but don't hold it against me. Please don't equate my last name, Rodriguez, with low intelligence or motivation. Don't look at my brown eyes and see an illegal immigrant who refuses to speak English preferring incomprehensible Español instead. Don't view my dark skin and black hair as exotic. Don't stereotype me as a Latin lover. Please don't judge me so readily. Others have done so too many times already. *Although for many people racism and discrimination are well-known but abstract issues, for me they have been a very personal concern which I have had to confront on a daily basis.*

Changes To Conclusion For Pomona's Question: "Pomona College defines diversity in broad terms including academic interests, ethnic background, educational opportunities, political views, socioeconomic environment, and personal pursuits among others. Reflect upon ways which you expect Pomona's diverse student body will affect your experiences inside and outside the classroom." *Changes are noted in italics.*

(Last Paragraph) Today I do more than complain about the misguided attitudes that people have. I show them to be in err. Through my achievements and work I challenge anyone who has doubts about my abilities. I will continue to work hard to achieve the good grades and accomplishments that I already have. *In an environment as diverse as at Pomona, I know that there will be others who will join me in my mission. I hope to learn from the ways in which they have dealt with similar problems and also that they will gain something from my experiences. Discrimination will not go away on its own, but that does not mean that we who are its victims must sit still.* I finally know what my mother meant in the front seat of our station wagon. If other people choose to stereotype me, so be it. It won't change anything for me. I am a Latina and I am proud of who I am. Yo soy latina.

From Anita's examples, you can see that it is possible to use the same essay to answer a number of questions. Anita was lucky since her original essay was easy to adapt to the various questions. Chances are that your essay will need a little more editing to make it fit. Also, since we don't have the space to reprint her essay five times keep in mind that we could only show you the *major* changes that Anita made.

When you begin to recycle, keep in mind that more important than *where* you add is *what* you add. Some essays are easy to recycle while others will require more work. But whenever you modify an existing essay to answer another school's question you are saving yourself a tremendous amount of time. Even if you have to tinker with a few sentences in each paragraph, it sure beats writing a whole new essay.

How To Shorten A Long Essay

There is nothing more frustrating than cutting, clipping, and reworking your essay for the 14th time only to find that it is still 126 words too long. When you are trying to trim a too-long essay, word or page restrictions can be an insufferable burden. You can cut a word here or scrap a word there, but it always seems that you need to do more.

In this section, you will learn some techniques for reducing a too-long essay. The key is that it is too slow and painstaking to clip word by word. To truly down size an essay, you must delete whole sentences and even paragraphs.

The first step to heavy duty slimming down is to read through your overweight essay and mark the key segments that are absolutely, without a doubt necessary. Among what's left look for parts of the essay that are not essential but merely add detail. (Do not look to eliminate single words—although if you find a word that you don't need, don't be afraid to give it the ax.)

Your goal is to divide your essay into sections that are absolutely essential and sections that can be discarded if necessary. To help separate the icing from the cake, ask yourself the following questions:

▶ What are the main ideas that you are trying to convey?

▶ If you delete this sentence will your idea still be coherent?

▶ Are the details in this sentence absolutely essential to the overall point? Can a phrase or two be eliminated?

▶ Is there a way to shorten the sentence and present the same information in fewer words?

When you have finished categorizing your essay, start eliminating the unnecessary parts. Keep asking yourself if the reader really needs the extra information.

It may be hard, but some of the best written sentences in your essay may only be adding detail that is not really necessary to advance the main point. You may be very proud of creating such wonderful prose, but remember that pride is one of the seven deadly sins. You need to eliminate these sentences, no matter how personally attached you feel to them, since they really are only overburdening your essay.

After you finish cutting, read your essay again (or better yet have someone else read your essay) to make sure that it does not sound choppy and that you have not inadvertently removed a critical piece of information. You may need to alter or add transitions between paragraphs.

If your essay is still too long, here are a few sneaky tricks:

▶ Decrease the side, top, and bottom margins.

▶ Decrease the line spacing from double space to 1.75 or 1.5.

▶ Make your font 11 points instead of 12. Note, however, that you should not go below 10 points since you don't want the admissions officer to need a magnifying glass to read your essay.

▶ If you need to exceed the page requirement try to do so by no more than half a page. Thus, for a 2 page essay you should try not to submit anything longer than 2 1/2 pages. (A page is usually considered to be 250 words.)

The following essay was a very detail-heavy one. It was written in response to the question, "Tell us about a significant or meaningful experience in your life." While the college allowed the author, Kyle, to add extra papers as necessary, the scholarship application for another school (which also asked about a significant experience) provided much less space. Note that to trim this essay, much of the detail was removed but the main ideas and emotional power were retained.

Ozzie Without Harriet (Condensed Version)

Note: Italicized sentences in parentheses are those that Kyle deleted.

I was eight years old when they told me. At the time I was wearing my Superman pajamas and was lying in bed waiting for my kiss good night. I could tell that something was wrong when my parents came into my room together. *(They looked like they were on parade, marching in one after the other. Only this parade had no music or cotton candy.)*

"Your father and I have something to tell you, Kyle," my mother said. *(For the first time she did not look at me as she spoke.)* "Your father is going to have to go away, and you are going to stay with me. We're getting a divorce."

Until that moment my concept of marriage and family had been based upon my favorite daytime rerun: Ozzie and Harriet. *(I looked forward with great anticipation to each Saturday's episode.)* Part of the show's appeal was that I would unconsciously impose the qualities of this *(black and white)* TV family upon my own and viewed them as a mirror of my parents and me.

Now with my whole world threatened *(with destruction)* I did not know how to react. I still recall, *(even to this day,)* that my first spontaneous thought when my parents made the announcement was: What's Ozzie going to do without Harriet?

("When will Daddy come back?" I asked my mother, who still did not look at me.)

("Kyle, he's not coming back. You will still see him on the weekends, but he's going to move away for good.")

From that night on I vowed never to forgive my parents and I promised myself that I would never again watch another episode of Ozzie and Harriet—*(feeling somehow that my TV family too had betrayed me.)* Life was not simple and families were no longer defined by two parents, children, and a house surrounded by a white picket fence.

It's amazing how the human mind deals with trauma and how quickly it tends to recover. Although initially shocked, sad, and angry I found, *(to my great displeasure,)* that I could not continue to be mad *(at my parents. Even though I felt that they were making a great mistake and were entirely insensitive to the wishes and desires of their only son, I could not maintain my depression.)*

About a month after my father moved out I visited him for the first time. I was amazed to see all of his belongings gathered in the small space of his new apartment. *(His electric shaver I used to pretend to shave with was on a tiny sink in an unfamiliar bathroom; the beat up fuzzy yellow chair I used to jump on was in a strange new living room on the 10th floor; and the picture of me in the macaroni frame I made in the first grade sat next to a bed in which my mother did not also sleep.)* I knew that these were his belongings, but I was not convinced that this was his home. I still imagined that his place was with my mother and me. With each visit, however, I came to realize that this was his new home.

As I grew older I learned the sad fact that divorce is not such an uncommon experience. More than a few of my friends had parents who were separated. However, I noticed that they often retained their anger and bitterness for far longer than I had. *(None certainly said that divorce had been good for them.)*

Was I odd? Not only did my bitterness wane after a few months but I also learned some things that made me realize that my parents' divorce was not necessarily such a bad thing.

This revelation came while talking to my mother over dinner one night. I had just entered high school and was brimming full of a premature sense of adulthood. We almost never talked about the divorce but for some reason on this particular night I asked my mother why she and my dad decided to end their marriage. I was amazed at how clearly my mother was able to lay out the reasons for their growing unhappiness with each other and how they mutually agreed after a long discussion that separation was the best option. *(Their reasons for divorce were not unusual—my parents just discovered things about each other that they did not like and as time went on their arguments became more frequent and their disenchantment grew deeper. As I* was going to sleep, *in the same bed I had been in when I was told of their divorce,)* I had a strange feeling in which a part of me was glad that my parents had separated rather than stayed in a situation where both were unhappy.

(My father has since remarried and seems to have a full life with his new family. He is still an important part of my life and I try to see him at least once a month—although my ever-increasing commitments to the tennis team and debate club have often made it difficult to find the time. My mother has not remarried but seems very content with her life and still stays in touch with my father and his family.)

(Perhaps I was lucky that my parents' divorce was amicable. I am sure others have experienced more bitter separations and therefore have not been able to overcome their animosity as easily. But I for one am glad to have been able to come to terms with the situation and see that all was not for the worst. With the talk these days of America's high divorce rate I wonder sometimes if we can say unequivocally that such is always lamentable. After all, divorce can mean the end to a union which is in a state of unhappiness. If this means two people have realized

that they have made a mistake and need to seek fulfillment elsewhere, then what is so wrong? Is it not better for people to admit their mistakes and move on rather than stay locked in a situation of perpetual unhappiness?)

Children of the divorced, like myself, are of course the hardest hit. And it's not easy to see the good behind what seems to be so obviously a mistake. *(Even I still harbor, deep down inside, a wholly unrealistic fantasy that someday my parents will reunite.)* I may not be as happy as I could have been had my parents had a good marriage. But they didn't have a good marriage and they are vastly happier now than before.

I have broken all of the vows I made on the night I learned of my parent's divorce. I no longer hate them. I no longer feel betrayed. And I have even watched Ozzie and Harriet since then. But this has only been possible since I now know that Ozzie without Harriet can be for the better.

To slim down his essay, Kyle eliminated a number of descriptive passages. However, he kept his key points: how he overcame the trauma of his parents' divorce and even found some good in it. By removing the extras, Kyle's essay loses some of its color, but it still has enough detail for the reader to be able to visualize and feel what he has experienced. This is the kind of balance that you want to achieve between over and under trimming.

How To Build A Longer Essay

It's a toss-up about which is more difficult: slimming down an essay or adding to one. Chances are you won't even encounter the second problem because, with the limited amount of space you have, it's just too easy to use it all up.

However, occasionally you may find that you have not written enough. If so, don't worry. Admissions officers have a reputation for preferring less to more. Case in point, Princeton's instructions for writing the essay contain this note: "Remember, Lincoln's Gettysburg Address was only 272 words."

If you only have 400 words for a 500-word essay and have nothing left to say, leave it. It's better to submit just 400 quality words than to add an additional 100 words of fluff.

Still, if you have a phobia of too much white space on paper or feel that there is something missing in your condensed work, there are a number of ways you can expand an essay.

One of the first things to do is add more detail. Try to include information that aptly portrays your physical environment: What can you see, smell, touch, or hear? What is the weather like? Is it hot? Humid? Freezing? What time is it? What are the people around you doing?

Try to also include more information about how you feel and why: What factors are influencing your emotions? What mood are you in? How do your emotions change throughout the essay? What is the history behind how you are feeling?

Another strategy is to take simple sentences and expand on them to create depth. Instead of saying, "I had never felt so sad in my life" you can change the sentence to read, "I had never felt so sad in my life but it was not because I lost the game; it was because I had done so in such a poor manner." In this case you not only double the length of the sentence but you also add more meaning and clarity. You don't want to do this for every sentence, but read through your work and find places where you can create depth of meaning.

When you do this, however, it is important to make sure that your main idea does not get lost in all of the added details and descriptions. You do not want to "pad" an essay with useless words. Still, almost every essay can be skillfully lengthened by adding relevant descriptions and detail. As a last resort, you can also fiddle with the margins or spacing a little but, be careful since you don't want the format of your essay to be distracting.

A Final Warning About Recycling

The greatest danger of recycling is that in the process of clipping and reworking, the original focus of your essay may become lost. To make sure that this does not happen, reread the question and your essay several times. Ask yourself: Does this essay truly answer the question? Remember that while you have the freedom to interpret the question in your own way, you do not want the admissions officers to wonder if you misunderstood it because your essay lacks focus and does not clearly state at the beginning how you intend to answer the question.

Here are some other important questions to ask yourself:

▶ Does the introduction set up the essay so that it is clear that you are trying to answer the stated question?

▶ Have you given too much or too little information or detail?

▶ Do the sentences and paragraphs flow together well?

▶ Are the transitions smooth and the connections between your ideas apparent?

▶ Is the logic of the essay preserved?

If you are unsure about your recycled work, get a second opinion. Have someone who has not read the original essay read the recycled essay to see if it is still clear and understandable.

Although recycling promises to produce an essay in a fraction of the time it took to write the original, careful attention still needs to be exercised especially when writing the introduction and conclusion. Your recycled work needs to be just as polished as the original essay.

As you recycle your various essays, the job will get easier. And don't forget when it is all over to congratulate yourself on having saved valuable time and effort.

EXAMPLE ESSAYS:
THE GOOD, BAD, & UGLY

● ●

In This Chapter

▲ **Learn From The Essays That Worked**

▲ **The Magnum Opuses: 14 Essays That Opened Ivy Gates**

▲ **7 Disastrous Essays That Spelled Rejection**

The College Essay In The Real World

After the last two chapters you probably have so many writing strategies, tips, *Do's,* and *Don'ts* swimming around in your head that you must be wondering just how it all comes together in a real essay.

In this chapter we will look at some real-life essays. Since this is intended to be an exercise in learning by example, you should pay attention to how each student has used the techniques in the previous chapters to craft his or her essay. When you write your essays you should use these examples as models to which to compare your own work.

We also have included some essays that were not so successful. While a few of these clinkers might have gotten "A's" in English class, all failed to make the grade with admissions officers. We hope that by reading these essays you will understand better what doesn't work and will not repeat the errors of past students.

Violating our own essay-writing rule of not using clichés, we must emphasize that college essays are like snowflakes: no two are alike. Each essay reflects the personality and character of the individual writer. Therefore, when considering how to use these essays in your own writing it is important that you only try to emulate the quality, enthusiasm, and creativity of the writers, but *not* their specific style, word choice, topic, or approach. Besides being plagiarism it is very unlikely that your personality and writing style matches precisely those of the authors.

Some years ago a student found a fantastic essay in a long out-of-print book on college admissions. Thinking that no one would remember this essay he copied it virtually word for word. A few months later he received what he thought was an acceptance letter. Instead, it was a letter from an admissions officer informing him that he had been the editor of that long out-of-print book. The letter promised that the student's plagiarism would be made known to other colleges. Apparently the admissions officer made good on his promise since this student was rejected by every school to which he had applied.

Each one of us has unique experiences, philosophies, outlooks, and styles. If you can convey some of yours on paper you will have an essay that is far superior to that of anyone else.

Do not take these essays as absolute symbols of perfection. Although they are superbly written and were critical to each student's admission into a top school, they still have areas that could use improvement. One week after I (Jim Good) submitted my Harvard essay, I realized that one section could have been made infinitely better with a few minor changes. As with all writing, no essay is ever completely finished.

Please also keep in mind that there are many ways to write a good essay, but unfortunately we only have space to print 14 samples. If the essay you are writing does not look like any of these essays that's fine! If you followed the rules and advice in Chapter 5 then you probably have a winning essay that is 100% original. Don't let these examples limit your imagination.

After each essay is a short analysis that highlights its strengths or weaknesses from the point of view of an admissions officer–which really is the only point of view that matters.

One last note: Some essays were submitted for a general "tell us something about you," topic while others were directed at more specific questions. Also, some colleges allowed the applicant to use several pages, while others only let them use one.

The Magnum Opuses: Essays That Opened Ivy Gates

These are the essays that worked to help their authors open the gates to America's elite colleges. As you read them, it will be apparent why they worked. All of them capture some part of the writers' personality, thoughts, and emotions. Seductively and creatively, they captivate the readers, creating in them a desire to learn more and to get to know the authors better. The writers carefully craft

> **Warning!**
>
> The following essays represent only a few of the many ways to write a good essay. Your own essay probably does not and should not look like any of the ones here. We give you these essays so you can see what has worked, but by no means should you force your essays to look like these examples.

their words, virtually constructing original pieces of art. Again keep in mind that your goal is to emulate their quality (not their words). We hope that these examples will serve as an inspiration for your own writing.

Laughter Is What I Like To Hear
• • • • • • • • • • • • • • • • • •

By: Laurie C.

It happens the same way every time. It begins with her head tilted at a slight angle, her hands resting on each hip, and her slightly abundant belly thrust forward. The first thing you notice is a shake beginning to run through her body. There is no audible counterpart until a fraction of a second later. Then, the sound follows. And what a glorious sound it is. It is hearty and natural and fills up every empty space in the room. It is full and beautiful, a melody to my ears. For as long as I can remember, I have been bathed in my mother's laughter.

One of my first recollections of my mother's laughter was when I brought home my 1st-grade report card. As my mother looked it over she began her ritual movement; tilted head, hands on hips, belly thrust forward. "All A's! It's time to celebrate!" she shouted, with the sound of her laughter shortly following. She whisked me off the ground and held me close as we danced around our kitchen cheek to cheek with both of our laughter thick in the air.

Since that first report card, every achievement has been celebrated with my mother's laughter. From my second all "A" report card to winning the potato sack race at the Girl Scout Jamboree to my first-place prize in the high school science fair to finally beating my rival from Smith High at the district track meet, my mother's laughter has been my most rewarding congratulations.

Although I am about to venture out into the world by myself, I still expect to share my mother's laughter. In the sunny Harvard Yard during commencement, above the pews of my church at my wedding, and by my hospital bedside after giving birth to her first grandchild. There is so much laughter that I have heard already in my short lifetime and so much more that I have left to hear.

My mother's laughter will always be a source of comfort and inspiration. Hearing it, I know that I have done well. When others who know my family tell me that I am just like my mother, I grow happy indeed. And then, I laugh just a little bit louder.

Comments On "Laughter Is What I Like To Hear"

A well-written and solid essay, Laurie takes a common subject and presents it in an original way. Laurie displays her writing skill through her excellent use of rich detail and creative language when describing her mother's laughter. You can almost hear it echo as you read her words.

Most important, Laurie's approach and style show that she is a mature and sensitive individual. We learn about Laurie through the moments in her life that she shares and by the fact that she hopes to carry on her mother's laugh. Laurie does not try to use fancy writing or embellish her narrative with unnecessary events. She writes an honest piece which says a lot about herself. Finally, Laurie's essay has the added advantage of being upbeat and positive as she shares with us her obviously strong relationship with her mother. This kind of positive attitude always reflects well on students.

Visiting Grandfather

• • • • • • • • • • •

By: Billy K.

Worse than movies about overgrown, blood-thirsty sharks; worse than ghost stories of night marchers coming to steal my soul; worse even than trips to a six-inch-long needle wielding doctor were my childhood visits to see grandfather. There was nothing that caused a greater amount of fear or consternation in my eight-year-old psyche than those simple words, "Billy, we're going to visit Grandfather." Not even, "Billy, it's time to take a bath" could come close.

Visits to see Grandfather were so dreadful because they meant going to his nursing home. For me there was something wholly terrifying about nursing homes and hospitals. Maybe it was the musty, mediciney odors that wafted through the halls. Or the wheelchair-bound people with eyes glazed over and bodies contorted in strange positions. Or maybe it was the sounds of ignored mumbling, crying, and moaning that echoed throughout the building. As a child, these were the scents, sights, and sounds that I remembered most poignantly.

My grandfather's room offered little safety. I knew that the man lying motionless in the hospital bed was family. But his frail body—I remember that his skin was so thin that every contour of his face was visible—and his inability to communicate more than a nod or unintelligible mumble made me look at him as if I were viewing an Egyptian mummy at a museum.

Since my grandfather passed away while I was still young, this was my lasting image of him—the frail, nearly petrified man lying on that horrible hospital bed in that terrible nursing home. But last Christmas this all changed because of a decision to make a booklet tracing the family tree as a gift to my mother.

As part of this project I found my grandfather's photo album. Out of habit I started from the back. The last page of pictures was of my grandfather in the hospital—just as I remembered him. As I flipped through the book from back to front, however, he grew younger. A picture of him posing with my mother when she was 16. Another of him in a crisp Navy uniform after returning from the Pacific. And finally, as a young man in his senior year wearing the jersey of an offensive lineman for Wilshire High. On his chest was printed boldly the number 28, his number—which was, coincidentally, now also mine.

As I looked at the pictures, I no longer envisioned the frail, motionless skeleton of a man who I thought of as my grandfather. Instead, I imagined the handsome young man posing with his baby daughter in front of his first house. I saw the confidence-inspiring face of a destroyer captain who coolly commanded his crew as they pursued enemy submarines. I imagined the high school senior with thick forearms that at one time had plowed through countless defensive lines. The man who I remember in the bed who never walked and hardly talked faded and was replaced by this new image.

Like my grandfather's life I hope to pass through time with something to be proud of at each moment. And I hope that when I am confined to a bed, my grandson will see me not for what I have become but for what I once was.

Comments On "Visiting Grandfather"

A super essay for a jock! Billy was an All-American football player but you wouldn't have known it from this essay. He is modest and reflective—hardly the stereotypical arrogant athlete that you might expect. Plus, you'd better believe that the admissions officers were happy they did not have to read another essay about how Billy won the "big game" or how important football had been to his life. Instead, the admissions officers were treated to a side of Billy's character that was nuanced, sensitive, and thoughtful. Not to mention the essay also demonstrates that Billy can write some decent prose.

Billy begins his essay with a strong introduction that piques the reader's curiosity about why he hated to visit his own grandfather. In his explanation Billy does not try to minimize or justify his childhood fears and anyone who has ever been to a nursing home would probably empathize with his feelings. The main body of the essay takes a depressing situation and shows how it was transformed through Billy's discovery of his younger grandfather. The only weakness of the essay is in the conclusion, which is somewhat disjointed and abrupt. It would have been better if Billy had developed it a little further. Nevertheless, this is a solid, honest essay that makes no pretensions and is a pleasure to read.

A Family Expedition
• • • • • • • • • • •

By: Samantha C.

Driving along the Columbia River gorge, moving 65 miles per hour toward Eastern Oregon from Portland I imagined we were the brave explorers Lewis and Clark. Only we were following their trail in reverse and in the comfort of an air conditioned mini-van chauffeured by my father.

It was summer and we were on our "family road trip." While I always add "family" before "road trip" I really should say "my father's road trip." He is the one who insists on driving, enjoys mapping out our route in great detail, and loves stopping at all the fast food pit-stops along the way. (I think he secretly looks forward to the greasy hamburgers and steaks that his health-conscious wife and three daughters rarely let him eat at home.) This year although the rest of us had wanted to fly to Orlando we nevertheless agreed, after our customary complaints, to once again go by car.

I wonder how often Lewis and Clark got lost? Probably quite often but then without a map and charting heretofore unexplored territory (at least by Europeans) they had a pretty good excuse.

My father, on the other hand, despite the numerous improvements in cartography that have occurred since the Lewis and Clark expedition, never fails to let us experience what it is like to be totally lost. This often happens on what he calls a "scenic route."

On this trip it occurred after we had passed the small town of Pendleton in Eastern Oregon. My father as usual had his set of USGS maps, which for those of you who do not know stands for U.S. Geological Survey and are highly detailed maps often used by forestry rangers, mountaineers, and my father. My mother, on the other hand, always gets a copy of the AAA map. So as we neared the designated point which my father had duly marked on his USGS map as our place of departure from the main road my mother, out of years of experience, pulled out her AAA map to confirm my father's "scenic route" plans.

"I don't see a road on this map," she announced.

"Sure, there is. I have it marked right here on the map," my father replied.

Of course, we in the back seat knew that they were looking at two different maps.

"No. Listen to mom!" we three sisters shouted just as our dad turned the van off the highway and on to a very unimproved gravel road.

I wonder how often Lewis fought with Clark over which way to go?

"Look at how beautiful the countryside is," my father exclaimed. Unfortunately there was so much dust being kicked up that everything looked hazy. My father tried to spray some water onto the windshield but only succeeded in creating mud.

Our narrow gravel road eventually turned into an even narrower dirt road.

"Sure is a bad road," my father said after the umpteenth bump had jarred us out of our seats causing my little sister to scream. Now when my father says something even remotely negative I start to worry.

"Turn around, turn around," we all shouted from the back seat.

Did Lewis ever tell Clark that he wanted to turn around?

My father is not one to concede easily. He shifted the van into its lowest gear. In the back we were already shifted around like popcorn as each rock, rut, and bump sent us and our luggage into the air. I was growing dizzy and my little sister appeared to be turning green. In the front my mother was trying to reason with my father, "The road is only going to get worse." "That map of yours is out of date." "We're going to get stuck out here." But to no avail.

My father has that pioneer spirit. However, things were going from bad to worse. The road was barely distinguishable from the surrounding prairie grass and the van was beginning to strain from climbing the hills. The back seat was total chaos. The cloud of dust in which we were traveling was quickly infiltrating the interior, causing my allergy sensitive sister to sneeze. My mother was now yelling at my father to turn around. My little sister was crying. My other sister was adding to my mom's admonitions between violent fits of sneezing. And me? I could only wonder what Lewis and Clark would have done if their wagon was in the same predicament.

Then all of a sudden the van stopped.

"Look," my father said softly. As we slowly turned our attention away from him and looked out the window we realized we were on a plateau overlooking a lush valley with not a single man–made structure in sight. And stretched out before us was no longer a road but untrampled, virgin prairie grass. The last trace of the road was 50 yards behind.

"Well, I guess this is the end of the road," my father laughed. We got out and huddled around each other taking in the view. It was absolutely gorgeous.

When we finally returned to the main highway it was late and we decided to stop at a local motel. After taking a shower and eating our standard greasy fare for dinner we all lay in our beds while my father peered over his maps planning our next "scenic" detour. Before I fell asleep my mind wandered upon Lewis and Clark one last time and I knew that for a few special moments I had known what it must have been like to discover an unspoiled vista.

Comments On "A Family Expedition"

Travel is a very popular topic for college essays. Most applicants try to tell too much. They try to compress a two-month tour of Eastern Europe into a single 500-word essay. It just doesn't work. Samantha has focused on just one small part of her family's summer trip. And it works very well. It is interesting and humorous. Notice that Samantha adds humor by simply drawing attention to what was naturally comical about the incident. Even if for some reason the reader does not find it funny, it is still an interesting story. Best of all, Samantha gives us a peek into her family. She shows us their idiosyncracies and how this created a memorable, and stressful, situation. Samantha also approaches the chaos of her family's road trip compassionately. No one is put down or lampooned and there is no uncalled-for sarcasm, which does not usually appeal to admissions officers.

Grandma And Grandpa's Living Room

By: Lisa L.

Every time I visited my grandparents' home, they sat in their own chairs—Grandpa in his cracked leather Lazy-Boy flipping through the channels with the remote, Grandma in her quilted chair, cigarette dangling between her frail fingers. The Lazy-Boy, worn yet comfortable from use, and the quilted chair, a mixture of fabrics and intricate stitches, were a source of security to me. They were visual monuments representative of my grandparents.

Even when his study light which usually illuminated the room allowing him to intently fill in the answers to a crossword workbook with his sketchy yet steady scrawls was turned off or the ashes from her cigarettes (which I truly detested but still accepted simply because they were a part of her) were cold, I still perceived their supportive presence in the room.

As I sat against one of the dark oak walls, I peered across the room to view a memorabilia of pictures. They were arranged into two sets. One, consisting of somewhat blurry black and white snapshots, held various poses of my mother, her older sister, and her younger brother.

In this group of dramatic photos, I was brought back to the past, a past in which my mother was a child, youth exuding from her dressed in cowgirl tap-dancing outfit with boots, ten-gallon hat, and bandanna or in her prom dress grinning anxiously and nervously as her date lightly held her hand or in her gleaming cap and gown peering at the world, her eyes filled with idealism and innocence. In this arrangement, I found a connection to those who meant the most to me, a link to my past, and a connection to my heritage.

The other set of pictures, intermixed with the first, yet easily distinguishable, consisted of color photographs. My grandmother proudly and joyously held me as a newborn, her first grandchild, her prized descendant. Laughing riotously, shrieking wildly, my grandfather bounced me lightly into the air. Comfortably seated on the couch between my two grandparents, our glowing beams were captured by the camera.

In this set of pictures lay the present, but more importantly, portended the future. Here, collected on the space of the wall, was my hope for a future of happiness. As I grew older, so my potential grew.

As I looked at these pictures, I grasped dearly onto my necessity for survival. For this, though meaningless to others, is my epitome. It is my past, my heritage. It is my future, the link that connects my family and me to the wider expanse of the world. Within this sanctity of my grandparents' living room, I gain security from my supportive family, understanding of my place and purpose in life, and tranquillity from the connections that it provides.

Comments On "Grandma And Grandpa's Living Room"

Whether it was Grandma's famous Dutch apple pie or Grandpa's arrowhead collection, almost everyone has fond childhood memories of their grandparents' homes. This essay not only taps directly into these feelings of nostalgia but it takes the level of analysis one step further by revealing how these feelings established a sense of generational connection and support. It is the well developed ideas behind this essay which make it so effective. Lisa is able to show herself as contemplative, intellectually capable, and secure in her place in life. Notice also the excellent use of word choice, which is a skillful blend of casual and formal vocabulary.

Wimbledon Champ
• • • • • • • • • •

By: Angela B.

I am standing in center court. As my name thunders over the loudspeaker, my followers erupt uncontrollably awarding me with a standing ovation. Dressed in their tidy uniforms, the judges hand me my silver trophy. It is almost as big as I am. Still, triumphantly I heave it over my head, holding it proudly as the victor at the same time that I am blinded by the flash of the cameras.

In my dreams I am the next Wimbledon champion, one of the greatest athletes in the world, and a symbol of strength, talent, and endurance. In reality, however, I am lucky to have my racket meet the speeding blur of yellow fuzz which my coach persists in trying to convince me is an actual tennis ball.

I began taking tennis lessons six months ago. Unfortunately, I can't say that I have discovered any latent talent, but I can say that I love the sport. Twice each week I join a dozen other younger and better tennis aspirants in learning the mysteries of connecting the racket to the ball. Equipped with my feather light shoes for bouncing, colorful polo shirt for athletic appearance, and logoed cap for good luck; I am a giant towering above my dozen elementary school aged classmates. Unfortunately, neither size nor style is an indication of mastery.

Take for instance a recent lesson. It consisted of learning how the different angles at which we grip our rackets change the direction of the ball. Not surprisingly, the theory behind which direction the ball should go and the reality of where my balls actually went did not coincide perfectly. That is assuming that my racket actually made contact with the ball in the first place, which was often not the case.

Needless to say, it was frustrating to watch as the 8- and 11-year-olds in my class effortlessly met the fuzzy yellow thing with their rackets creating that satisfying "pop." I often wonder if there has been a genetic mutation in the past 10 years which enhances children's natural racket swinging ability which I somehow missed out on.

Still, despite my lack of coordination at times, the desperation I feel when my classmates easily master the strokes I only dream of attempting, and the sympathetic looks that my coach gives me, I love playing. I have felt no greater satisfaction than the first time I hit the ball across the net or the first time the ball actually remained within the confines of the court. And I have felt no greater pride than when my coach said, "Good job," and actually meant it or when my classmates selected me second to last instead of my standard last place for a round robin rally. I may not be the best tennis player, but I am proud of myself because I am trying. Wimbleton cup or not, this to me is the true essence of victory.

Comments On "Wimbledon Champ"

Most essays on sports showcase the mastery that the writer has achieved. Angela, however, writes about something she is not good at—in fact she sounds absolutely terrible at tennis. But being bad at tennis does not mean that she is a failure. In fact, the inner strength that she shows by persisting with the sport even though her lessons are a humbling experience demonstrates an incredible tenacity. This essay works because it is positive, expresses Angela's feelings honestly and without affected histrionics, and amuses the reader with a story they want to finish.

Kidney
• • • •

By: Mark A.

Would you like to buy one of my kidneys? How about a piece of my liver? I'd offer you my heart if I could. What? You don't want them? You are appalled that I would even consider selling a few of my organs? Would it make a difference if I told you that I need the money to put myself through school? No? Well, what is wrong with selling a few of my not so "vital" organs? They are, after all, mine.

Disgusting? Degrading? Well, who are you to tell me what I can do with my body? Unless maybe you are an advocate of some form of slavery where one human being is able to own another. That is what you are implying, right? That you (or your laws) can forbid me to dispose of my body (or at least a part of it) as I please is tantamount to claiming some right to it, is it not? If I truly am free and if I do "own" myself—and everything inside—then why can't I choose what to do with it?

Human decency? I've heard that argument before. You think that by affixing a price to myself and placing my body parts on the open market that I am devaluating all human beings. That's just not true!

How much is a human being? What kind of question is that? I don't know. You can't put a price on human life. But I'm not selling my life just some organs. I suppose that by offering to sell a piece of me I might be contributing to the commodification of the human body. But I still don't see how what I am doing is so harmful.

Ok. So maybe you're right in saying that if many people did what I am doing there would arise a market for human body parts. Yes, I suppose some sort of trading would occur with a fluctuating price determined by supply and demand. But that's capitalism.

Yes. Brokers in body parts would probably emerge. And you might not be wrong in predicting that newspaper business sections would start to print the price of lungs and kidneys along side the day's exchange rates and price of pork bellies. I suppose that would be somewhat degrading.

I guess my actions do contribute to making our bodies more objectified. Certainly if everyone were like I am there would be no such thing as organ donation—only organ sales. Ok. I've heard enough. You sure do talk a lot. I guess I won't sell some of my organs. But say, do you have any ideas on how I can pay for my tuition?

Comments On "Kidney"

This is an offbeat and slightly risky essay that paid off. It was not the only essay that Mark submitted and was designed to complement another essay he wrote in which he talked about his work with Amnesty International (a human rights organization) and a suicide hotline. Since that essay was very serious Mark wanted to show a little of his creative side by addressing the real issue of a person's right to sell his or her organs through a fictional dialog.

The first few lines of this essay certainly capture your attention. Mark also clearly demonstrates that he knows the positions for and against the sale of organs. A creative essay like this is not easy to write, but if you can your essay will certainly stand out.

Dad's Pancakes
● ● ● ● ● ● ● ● ●

By: Jim G.

In spite of the various extracurricular activities I've done and interesting people I've met, not one event or person has been more meaningful to me than my father's preparation of breakfast.

Every morning I wake up to the sounds of my father cooking breakfast. While lying in bed, I try to guess if the clank of a pan means scrambled eggs or maybe his specialty, banana pancakes. Waking up to nearly 7,000 such mornings, I have grown to admire my father's dedication, a dedication which never falters even after hours of late night work.

I readily applied this value of dedication when I was elected Vice-Chairman of the State Student Council. With the tremendous amount of work related to this position, there were numerous occasions when I found myself having to choose between reviewing Board of Education policies and going to the beach with friends. And whenever I felt myself beginning to vacillate, I was always reminded of my father's unwavering dedication. I knew that the students who elected me depended on my dedication, and like my father's daily commitment, I would not let them down.

Whenever I hear my father making breakfast I always hope that he is preparing his piece dé résistance, banana pancakes. My father's pancakes are not generic "Bisquickies," but one-of-a-kind masterpieces. He uses scratch ingredients from hand sifted flour to home-grown bananas. As I grew older I noticed that I also began to assume the same ambition toward life as my father has toward his pursuit of the perfect pancake.

In my freshman year I took an interest in film making and soon my goal was to own a video camera and recorder. To accomplish this goal I could either wait six months until Christmas and hope Santa could afford a new VCR, or I could earn the money and buy it myself. My ambitious yearning took over and for the next three months of summer vacation I held a brush in one hand and a can of latex in the other as the hired painter of my grandmother's house. Although the work was hard and tiring, by the end of the summer, I was able to earn the money to fulfill my goal. Having learned from my father to strive for success, I have since worked fervently but patiently to attain my goals in life.

After my father has flipped the last pancake, the best part of breakfast has arrived—consumption. As I devour the stack of scrumptious pancakes, I notice that my father has a bright smile across his face; I am not the only one to savor this moment. My father truly enjoys making my breakfast. My father's joy from even the simplest things has been the model which I have tried to apply to my life every single day.

Failure to heed my father's lesson was disastrous in my sophomore year when I decided it would be impressive to become a cross country runner. As I was running the three mile course, I began to realize around the second mile that I did not particularly enjoy running. In fact I hated running. This painful experience reminded me of my father's overarching aim to enjoy what he is doing. Since then I have chosen to excel in tennis and other activities, not for the prestige or status, but simply because I enjoy them.

My father completes the tradition of preparing breakfast by soaking the dirty pans in the sink. As he does, I think of how fortunate I am. Some people only have one meaningful event in their lives, but I have one every single morning.

Comments On "Dad's Pancakes"

The "My Dad Is My Hero" essay is very popular and for it to work you need to insure that it is unlike any of the thousands of others which will be written. For example, many essays will talk about a father's commitment to his child's happiness by always "being there." But how many will explain how a father's making of breakfast has changed a life? Finding an original angle takes a lot of time, but if you can do it you will have won half the battle. This essay is also effective because it weaves the events of Jim's life into the narrative. We learn some very interesting things about him, and while this essay is ostensibly about his father we come away knowing more about Jim. Remember, it is always to your advantage to make sure your essay says something about you even if your topic is about someone else.

Hawaii
• • • •

By: George B.

When I sat down to write this essay about what individual has influenced me the most, a long list of potential candidates came to mind. I'm sure many applicants will write (and with good reason) that their parents or teachers or coaches were very influential in their lives. But, for me, after thinking long and hard I have come to the conclusion that no living individual has affected my life more than the island on which I live.

Growing up on this remote speck in the Pacific I came to think that the longest it took to get anywhere by car was an hour and a half. I assumed that summer, winter, spring, and fall denoted only minor changes of a few degrees in the daily temperature. And I certainly believed that Santa Claus arrived by boat and entered my chimney-less home through our unlocked window.

But more than these circumstantial influences of living on a 60 mile-wide island is the effect (directly and indirectly) that it has had on shaping who I am. In this essay I would like to share with you three of the most significant factors: the sun, ocean, and rocks.

The sun. One constant in Hawaii is the sun. Never allowing a change of more than a few degrees throughout the year, the sun seems to moderate any attempt by nature to cause a sudden seasonal change. I do not know if science would support my belief, but I am convinced that this lack of temperamental weather and drastic seasonal change has unconsciously seeped into my own nature. Rarely do I suddenly swing from calm to upset, happy to angry. Like the steady rays of the sun my personality is rarely jarred.

Testing such a hypothesis has been easy. Last year, for instance, I spent over a month constructing a cardboard model of turn of the century San Francisco as part of my final project in AP history. Building the model actually took longer than writing the report, but when I was finished I had what must have been the most realistic and accurate 3D scale model of downtown San Francisco ever produced by a high school junior. The day before I was to turn in my project I came home from school and was greeted at the door by my mother. "I'm really sorry but something terrible has happened," she said seriously. She led me into the den where I saw my so recently finished project sitting on the floor in shambles.

Apparently my four-year-old brother had decided to pit GI Joe against the Power Rangers for control of the city. In the fracas, many of the building got bent, a few were torn in half, and I think he even stepped on one section of the model flattening an entire block. I was stunned but right away realized that getting mad would not fix what had been done and that I had to think of some way to save my project. So I called my brother down from his room and had him help me destroy the rest of the buildings that were still standing. After we were done I printed out a new label for the model which simply said, "San Francisco After The Great Earthquake." Not only did my project get an "A" but I was complimented for such a dramatic presentation of the effect of nature's destructive force.

Of course, I hope this doesn't leave the impression that I am emotionless. I do sometimes get angry, just as even Hawaii suffers an occasional hurricane.

The ocean. From a very early age I have been enthralled by the beauty of the Pacific. Who would not want to explore its rich depths teeming with life of unimaginable form and beauty? Yet the perils— riptides, sharks, and moray eels—kept me away from descending beneath its surface. Although I often swam in the protective shallows near the shore, the thought of heading past the boundary of the reef terrified me.

But it seems even the ocean itself was out to tempt me. One day I went to an exhibit on undersea exploration and as luck (or fate) would have it won a special drawing for free scuba lessons. So, on the appointed day I donned a loaned wet-suit and strapped on my tank. I only realized after I had spent one of the most exciting hours of my life observing some of nature's most spectacular sights that I had also just conquered one of my greatest fears. Now I enjoy being a modern day Magellan as I probe the reefs in search of hidden passages or sneak up on a school of a thousand stick fish, their long, slender bodies motionless until through some intuitive sense the whole group decides to take a collective pulse forward. This is something that had I let my fears control me I would never have been able to witness. The ocean has shown me that my fears can be overcome.

The rocks. It may be hard to imagine that rocks can have any influence on a person's life, unless they want to be a geologist, but for me the rocks of Hawaii have helped create a special bond with my father. One day while my father and I were driving along a sugar cane field, we noticed a pile of rocks. It came from a turn of the century irrigation ditch and was originally used as a lining for a water flume.

But the most amazing thing was that the rocks had been carefully cut into precise squares. The time and skill it must have taken to cut each stone was remarkable.

Since these stones had been abandoned to make way for a newer concrete irrigation ditch, my father and I decided that to leave them would be a tragic waste. Since each rock weighed between 75 and 100 pounds, we could only load a few into the car at a time. Each day for a whole month my father and I would drive up after he came home from work and load a few stones into the car. It was a kind of bonding experience for my father and me. As we drove the half-hour to get the rocks we would talk about the day's happenings and once there we would admire the craftsmanship of the unknown stonecutters.

That event marked the beginning of other father-son projects. The next was to do something with all the rocks that were now piled in our yard. We decided to make a patio. Now each time I step out onto the patio I am reminded of how many ways the rocks have made my relationship with my father richer.

I don't suppose many of the essays you have read today have thanked an island for the influence it has had on someone's life. But for me the island of Oahu has certainly influenced who I am in countless ways. The sun, ocean, and rocks have left their indelible marks on my life, and it will be with a lot of sadness and a little trepidation that I leave my island home. When I do I will be sure to take some things with me as a reminder of where I came from: the multi-colored shell which I found on my very first dive and a piece from the rocks that my father and I used to make our family's patio. As for the warm rays of the sun which last throughout winter, I make no promises but I'll try to bring them along too.

Comments On "Hawaii"

If you read carefully the chapter on recycling you may have noticed that this is a recycled essay. The introduction and conclusion were tailored to fit the question, but the body was lifted almost word for word from another college essay that George wrote. Ironically, part of what makes the essay interesting is that it answers the question in an unusual and certainly unique way. George was lucky that this college gave him an unlimited amount of space. Ordinarily an essay like this should be shortened.

Nerd
• • •

By: Dave B.

I am a computer nerd. I have a subscription to *PC Magazine* and I stay up all night reading online articles about ISDN, EIDE, and SCSI (pronounced scuzzy). I can scan your picture and with a few clicks of the mouse give you a totally new hair style or create a custom database that will automatically compose and print personalized Christmas cards in December and thank-you cards in January. Yet, in spite of my love for computers and technology and all that is high-tech, my most passionate hobby may surprise you.

I love to sew.

In particular I make men's neck ties. I learned to sew from my grandmother while I was still in elementary school. At that age I was not yet immature enough to think that sewing was only for girls. I was fascinated at the way in which my grandmother worked her machine, taking various shapes of cloth and adeptly assembling them into beautiful shirts and pants and, once in awhile, a cowboy vest or two. One day my grandmother let me use her machine to connect two pieces of fabric. I was hooked. Every weekend I practiced sewing—usually making little bags to hold my toys.

I was learning how to make shirts when I entered junior high school and finally gained the immaturity that led me to quit sewing for a while. But, during the summer before 10th grade I found myself in need of money to fund my burgeoning interest in computers. When I told my grandmother my dilemma she suggested that I try making neck ties.

And so began a period of research and development that two months later resulted in the founding of my own tie making company as well as taught me the power of economics to overcome stereotypical roles. Financed by a $100 no-interest loan from my parents, Pacman Ties began operation. Our first line was, not surprisingly, blue cotton ties upon which I had silk-screened yellow Pacmen and multi-colored ghosts. They were an instant success—at least among my relatives. Their enthusiasm and my satisfaction from actually producing a useful product with my own hands led me to expand.

First production was systemized like an Intel assembly line to promote worker efficiency. This meant that my brother Brad got assigned the job of cutting all of the material for the ties using a state-of-the-art plastic pattern and fabric knife. Next, my sister Cynthia folded and ironed the fabric into the rough shape of the tie around another advanced tool: a pattern made from a pizza box. Finally, I took the shaped material and sewed the points and basted the back by hand.

During its first year Pacman Ties produced a variety of styles using exotic fabrics from around Seattle. But I was most proud of our video game inspired collection. Each tie was hand screened with images closely but not exactly resembling some of the year's most popular video games. They were not the most outstanding sellers, but they were certainly my favorite for their artistry. Pacman Ties sold mostly at craft fairs and swap meets and we built up a fairly loyal clientele. A year from when my grandmother suggested the idea of making ties I had made enough of a profit to buy my first personal computer.

As I was walking through the mall on my way to the computer store I had to pause in front of a display. For a long moment I seriously reconsidered purchasing the computer for in the window of a fabric store stood a gleaming new Singer sewing machine.

Comments On "Nerd"

The strength of this essay lies in the interesting story that Dave has to tell. While Dave might have mentioned in his application that he was the founder of Pacman Ties he certainly would not have had room for an explanation. Thus, Dave wisely uses the essay to showcase this unique personal accomplishment. If you have started a business, founded a club, or have an unusual hobby, the essay is a perfect place to highlight that accomplishment. But don't focus on the dry details of what you have done. Instead, explain why you did what you did and what motivated you to do it. This will help to convey your personality along with the details of your accomplishment.

Since Dave was applying to an elite technical school, it helped that he was able to display another (non-science) side of his personality. It would not be unimaginable that after reading his essay the admissions officers started to refer to Dave as "the tie man," thus making him unforgettable.

Dear Roomie
• • • • • • • •

By: Charissa Y.

Dear Future Roomie,

I am very eager to meet you, and knowing that we will be spending the year together, I thought that you should know a little more about the person with whom you are going to share a bunkbed and bathroom. But instead of writing a traditional, perhaps boring, letter I'd like to share with you what I consider to be the perfect illustration of my personality—the contents of my wallet. So let me take you on an adventure-filled guided tour of my wallet.

Safely protected between two strips of lamination is my *Rhino Club Card*, a cheesy remnant of a student leadership conference. Boldly printed on the front of the card is the Rhino Creed: "I am a Rhinoceros. I am full of Rhino energy and I can't wait to get up in the morning to start charging." Please don't think that your new roommate is a lunatic, but every morning I have stood in front of the bathroom mirror and recited the *Rhino Creed*. Not only have I used the Rhino Creed to energize my tired body, but I have also used it in times of stress.

I remember one of my most trying days, when in strict accordance with Murphy's Law everything which could go wrong did. That day was so stressful that I almost called my mother to take me home, but instead of succumbing to the pressure, I went to the bathroom, whipped out my Rhino card and repeated the Creed three times. Understandably, I got a few strange looks from other students, who were perhaps not as well versed in the Rhino creed, but when I left the bathroom, I felt like I was in control again. I got through that day thanks to my Rhino card, which is always safely secured in my wallet. As my roommate you are of course welcome to borrow it at anytime!

Folded evenly in half behind my Rhino card I keep my blood donor's certificate. Although donating blood for most people is not a big deal, for me it was a test of will power in overcoming a great fear. Since childhood I have had an extremely weak stomach for the sight of blood. In my freshman year I had to watch a movie about facial reconstruction. When it reached the actual surgery, I had to leave the classroom quickly and spend the next 20 minutes regaining my composure with my head between my knees. (I am certainly not going to become a pre-med.)

So, when the Red Cross came to set up our school's blood drive, I was faced with the challenge of confronting my psychological fear of blood. I decided to confront my fear and was ironically placed first in line. As I lay on the cot, I began to envision myself losing consciousness, rolling off the bed, ripping the needle out of my arm, and spraying blood across the school library. I blocked these thoughts and started to concentrate on something a little less gory, what I had just learned in math class. I had barely finished recounting logarithms when the nurse leaned over and said I was through. Although she told me that I might feel a little fatigued, I felt energized from my accomplishment. I have since kept my blood donor's certificate as a reminder of my personal victory over fear.

Hidden behind my driver's license and library card is a 1905 Buffalo nickel which I found when I was a child. When I found the nickel I was fascinated that something from so long ago could last so long. I then began to imagine the history behind the nickel. How many hands had it passed through and how many products had it purchased? I suppose that was the beginning of my interest in history.

Since then I have taken as many history classes as I could possibly fit into my schedule. I am now more intrigued not so much by the physical aspects of the past but by the social, political, and economic ideas of the time. I sometimes dream about what it must have been like to live during the American Revolution, Industrial Revolution, or Civil War. I have kept my buffalo nickel as a reminder of where my interest started.

I hope that you now know a little more about me (and still want to live together). Although there are many more facets to my personality as you will discover, I have shared what I thought were some of the most significant. I'd like to close with just one warning: Although my wallet is always filled with a lot of mementos, the one thing it always lacks is money.

Comments On "Dear Roomie"

Who wouldn't want to have a roommate this personable? Charissa takes a fresh approach to what can be a tired letter to a future roommate. Instead of merely describing who she is, she creatively uses the objects in her wallet as a segue into the personal stories of her life. She is also honest and not afraid to expose some of her most private idiosyncracies.

My Voice
• • • • •

By: Lisa L.

I have a soft voice. When I was younger, I did not like to present oral reports to my class because my voice did not carry. I have always desired a powerful voice, a voice which beckoned others to listen, which captivated them and provoked them into absorbing the thoughts which I expressed.

I was not born with this voice.

For this reason, I have turned to writing. For me, my voice is projected through the words I write. Since I wrote my first article for my elementary school newspaper at the age of eight, I have had a passion for journalism.

Through my school newspaper, *Aspects*, I grew acquainted with the field of journalism. As the Editor of this self-funded work, I learned the steps necessary to produce a publication—from the conception of articles to the distribution of the paper.

This background with *Aspects* developed in me the desire to continue my growth as a journalist. For this reason, I plan to develop my communications abilities in college as well as to write for a publication upon my graduation. With this education at Harvard and Radcliffe, I hope that my writing skills will progress in order to prepare for my future in the field.

With this education, I hope to hone my voice. I want others to listen, to hear my ideas, to have their lives affected by the articles that I write. For while the words that I speak are heard only once, the words that I write will be heard many times. Now, I have a powerful voice.

Comments On "My Voice"

This essay works because it not only explains the ambitious career goals of Lisa but also reveals something about her personality. The reader learns that while Lisa is not a vocally aggressive person, she is aggressive through her writing. It takes a lot of courage and self-confidence to admit to an Ivy League college that you are soft spoken—an attribute not usually seen as positive. However, after reading Lisa's essay you certainly don't feel that she is a passive person. This essay also illustrates that when writing an essay about your career goals, you should focus not only on those goals but also on yourself.

Why I Like To Lick Stamps
● ● ● ● ● ● ● ● ● ● ● ● ● ● ●

By: Jeremy M.

On the last day of every month I have the bland job of licking an entire roll of stamps, and even though this assignment is without much flavor I am never happier. Licking stamps is just one of the many tasks I do as founder, editor, writer, and publisher of "Vermont Sporting News," a statewide monthly newsletter dedicated to promoting outdoor activities such as hunting, fishing, and wildlife conservation.

Starting my own business was probably the most difficult thing I have ever attempted. Initially I had to deal with skepticism from my friends and family, who thought that this was too big of a project for a mere high school student. Then I had to formulate a plan to attract subscribers and manage the financial aspects of the business. Even after I successfully accomplished these tasks, my problems were not over, for I still had to find time to research, write, and publish each month's newsletter with a staff of one.

Looking in retrospect at all the lessons I have learned, I feel that there is one which underscores the rest: the importance of enjoying my work. "Vermont Sporting News" is a success because it allows me to combine my interest in outdoor activities with my love of writing. Because of this interest and love, I am able to make time to complete each month's issue. In fact the greatest reward for my efforts came not when I first turned a small profit, but when I received a letter from a subscriber which began with "Dear Staff..." and ended with "Keep up the good work." I had to chuckle to myself; after all, I am the staff and for me this job is as much pleasure as it is work.

Comments On "Why I Like To Lick Stamps"

In the limited space that many colleges allow for describing an extracurricular activity, Jeremy does a good job of engaging the reader with his creative introduction and then explaining the reasons why he has devoted a lot of time to his business. Notice also that his business is not successful in terms of money, but this is precisely what makes Jeremy all the more impressive. He clearly holds an alternative meaning of success that is far more noble that just making money.

Let It Snow
• • • • • • •

By: Mari K.

With so little snow, it was difficult to sculpt a snow creature in our backyard. Still, it was the first time that I, at the age of three, and my sister Patti, at the age of three months, experienced a "white Christmas" or even snow at all.

Because I have lived in California for most of my life, snow is an unfamiliar phenomenon to my siblings and to me. For this reason, I would like to pursue photography while at Harvard and Radcliffe.

I was ten years old when I received my first camera, a simple yet reliable Vivitar. With this camera, I photographed my father opening the water gun he received for his birthday, Uncle Matthew's new dogs —McGoo and McGrowlski—and my friend Dalila frolicking in the water after our elementary school graduation.

At the age of 14, I received a second, more advanced camera as a present. With this, I continued recording the events of my life. In the pictures that I took, my friendships grew stronger, my sister taller, my parents a bit older. With my pictures I traveled—to the beaches of Hawaii, the Mall of Washington, D.C., and Seattle's Space Needle.

Photography is truly a gift. It enables me to record events on film which would have become blurred images in my mind. At Harvard and Radcliffe, I would like to pursue photography in order to share this present with my family. For although my parents have seen snow maybe once or twice in their lives, my sister has only seen it at the age of three months and my brother never has. I would like to share with my family the scenery of the East, the people around me, and the school which I attend.

Although my family will be unable to be with me at Harvard and Radcliffe, I would like to be able to bring to them through photographs a bit of my way of life and as the Christmas song goes, "Let it snow, let it snow, let it snow."

Comments On "Let It Snow"

The mistake that most students make when describing their favorite extracurricular activity is that they *only* describe the activity, forgetting to describe themselves. This essay on photography works because Mari chooses to focus (no pun intended) on herself. The writing is sophisticated and the reader can easily envision all of the moments that Mari has captured on film. This gives the admissions officers a more complete picture of who she is (pun intended this time).

Losing A Bet Can Be Good
● ● ● ● ● ● ● ● ● ● ● ● ● ●

By: Greg K.

To an 11-year-old boy, *The Boy Scout's Handbook* is like a bible. Inside this half workbook half textbook are 20 different areas of study. Each area has several requirements which must be completed before earning a merit badge for that discipline. A parent's signature on the last page of each section signifies proof of completion. The average scout will finish one or two badges a month. As a young and already overambitious scout, I was intent on earning five. Also, I had the added incentive of a wager with my best friend.

As the month progressed, I passed the requirements for an Engineering badge, Fitness badge, Swimming badge, and Drama badge. All I needed was one more to complete my goal, but time was running out. On the night before our troop meeting I still had one requirement to fulfill before I could earn a Citizenship badge: I had to memorize not only the National Anthem but also the preamble to the Constitution.

As the night grew later and my eyes heavier, I realized that I was not going to be able to finish. I was then faced with a choice: succumb to failure and lose the bet or forge my mother's signature and earn what I would have rightfully earned if given only one more day. The choice was not easy, after all I was just a pen mark away from fulfilling my goal. But then I began to think about how much the badge and bet were really worth. I grudgingly concluded that lying, which was counter to everything the Boy Scouts represented, was not worth a silly medal or a stupid bet.

I did not achieve my goal of five badges and consequently lost the bet with my friend. But I maintained my honesty. Although I cannot say that *The Boy Scout's Handbook* has been the only thing that has tested my honesty, it did force me to make a decision about my integrity at an early age. Although I have long quit scouting I can still recite the scout pledge which begins with, "To be honest..."

Comments On "Losing A Bet Can Be Good"

Greg utilizes a short space wisely by presenting a dilemma that he faced as a child and that still influences him today. It helps that he is honest in his essay, admitting that naturally he was tempted to do the wrong thing. Surely many of the admissions officers could relate to similar situations in which they had to make a choice between what they wanted to do and what they should do. It also helps that although Greg writes about a moral issue, he does not preach. This is not a story about how "everyone should be honest" or how "honesty would make the world a better place." Greg tells a simple story about one event in his life where he made the right choice. He stays focused on the story and resists making general morality statements which would only detract from the narrative and give him an air of self-righteousness.

7 Disastrous Essays That Spelled Rejection

Here's a pop quiz: If we are trying to show you how to write a successful college essay, why would we print essays that failed? One answer: It's great entertainment during what can be an ugly and stressful time. The real answer: These essays demonstrate what does *not* work. By reading them, you will know better what sorts of essays turn admissions officers off, cause their eyes to glaze over, and send them into a deep slumber. In this way, the essays that did not work can be even more illustrative than those that did.

To give you a taste of what to expect, here are some of what we like to call "Dumbo Leads." These are real-life openings written by students. Right away you can tell that the essay is going to be boring or worse.

My name is…

The other day my probation officer said …

Please let me into your school!

I want to go to Harvard because… (written on a Yale application)

Pee Wee Herman is one of our nation's greatest political heroes.

I think applying to college is like sitting on a big toilet...

And now, ladies and gentlemen, boys and girls, for your further entertainment and education, the essays that failed. Warning: Some of these essays are truly painful to read.

My Wish To End Homelessness
● ● ● ● ● ● ● ● ● ● ● ● ● ● ● ● ● ●

By: Keith M.

If I had only one wish in life, I would wish to end homelessness in the world. In America, homelessness is one of our biggest problems.

There are simply too many people without a place to live, without food to eat, and without clothes to ward off the winter wind. It is to help these huddled masses that I would like to fulfill my wish.

I first learned of the plight of the homeless last Thanksgiving when my Social Studies class took a trip to our city's homeless shelter to help serve meals. It was one of the most eye–opening experiences I ever had. Before, I had never been to a homeless shelter. I had never touched a homeless person or even talked to one. The only homeless people I knew were the ones who held the signs at the side of the freeway saying "Will Work for Food" or who asked if I could spare a quarter. But here I was confronted with the stark reality of the evils in our country. Seeing how these people really lived changed my life completely.

After going to the homeless shelter last year, I realized that homeless people are human beings. They have feelings and they have dreams. They need to eat and sleep and deserve to at least have a roof over their weary heads.

It is my greatest dream to solve the homeless problem. I think that there are many things that we can do to address this issue if only every person in American would take just a moment to realize the depth of this problem. Together we can work to find a solution.

Homeless people need food, clothes, shelter, and work. If only we can meet these simple, basic human needs we could, in a single day, wipe out the problem of homelessness.

We truly need to work together as human beings on our shared Planet Earth to make sure that every person has a home.

Comments On "My Wish To End Homelessness"

Keith writes what we call the "Miss America" essay. Like contestants in the Miss America pageant, Keith professes in a melodramatic and overly emotional tone a desire to solve a serious social problem which clearly cannot be easily resolved. Notice that Keith never mentions what he has done since discovering the plight of the homeless nor does he even try to expound on his vague idea of a solution. This essay reveals either his naivete or simply a lack of effort to consider his topic carefully.

At all costs, avoid writing a "Miss America" essay. Do not write about your plan to personally end worldwide problems such as war, hunger, or poverty. Do not write about your life long dream to hug every child, to stop gang warfare, or to quell the drug trade. These are the unrealistic and trite wishes that Miss America wannabes robotically repeat. While these can be excellent topics, if you choose them, keep your essay focused and centered on what you have done. It's okay to mention your dream for a better tomorrow. Just don't make it your whole essay. Also note that Keith shamelessly steals well-worn phrases from such places as the Statue of Liberty. Get some originality!

My Achievements
● ● ● ● ● ● ● ● ● ●

By: Kevin W.

There are many things that I have done that I am proud of. Throughout high school I have done well academically and socially. I think that my achievements portend what I will accomplish in college. Please allow me to describe some of my successes.

First, when it comes to academics, I have excelled. Throughout high school, I have maintained a 4.0 grade point average while taking challenging classes such as Advanced Placement biology and Advanced Placement English. I also studied Latin for two years and math for all four years. My teachers have always said that I am an excellent student, and I will work hard to get good grades in college, too. I also scored 1450 on the SAT.

I have participated in a number of enjoyable activities in high school. I played the clarinet in the school band for three years. I volunteered at the local hospital for one summer. I also was a member of the Tennis Club and the tennis team for two years. In college, I plan to join many clubs and organizations as well. I will probably join the band and would like to play on the tennis team.

In high school I have also won numerous awards. For example, I won first place in the science fair last year. I won an Outstanding

Writing Award from my ninth grade English teacher. I also earned a letter by being on the tennis team.

During the past two years I have also worked part-time at a clothing store in the shopping mall. This experience has taught me much about what it is like to work hard and long hours. While I certainly do not want to make this a career, I am glad to have had the experience.

Last, I have a very nice personality. Many people say I am thoughtful and kind. I enjoy being nice to others, especially those who are less fortunate than I am. I think I would be a great addition to your college. I have achieved a lot, and I plan to achieve a lot more in the future.

Comments On "My Achievements"

Instead of writing an essay, Kevin writes an expanded resume. Although he is rightfully proud of his accomplishments, his essay tells us little more about his personality than what we already know from his application. Kevin also seems to be concerned with bragging about his accomplishments, about making sure that the admissions officers will not overlook all the wonderful things that he has done. It's too bad, however, that this is not what the admissions officers want to see in the essay.

Never offer a laundry list of your achievements, no matter how incredible they may be. Also, don't write about information that is found elsewhere in your application, unless you plan to elaborate on an interesting aspect about it. Finally, notice that Kevin's essay looks like it could have been written in an hour. There is no originality or even attempt to correct obvious mistakes.

Harvard Is Perfect For Me
• • • • • • • • • • • • • •

By: Missy S.

I have dreamed all of my life of going to Harvard. I think that it is the perfect college for me and that I would fit in wonderfully.

First of all, the environment of your college is incredible. Harvard Square that surrounds the campus is always alive with a mix of interesting people. Last summer I visited Harvard and enjoyed watching a magician, juggler, and other street performers. Harvard is also close to Boston, one of the most charming and historical cities in America. I love walking the Freedom Trail and seeing the sites of our country's important historical events.

In addition to the surroundings of Harvard, the campus itself is beautiful. Last summer the trees were full with leaves, and students peacefully relaxed in the Yard. Some tossed frisbees while others read or sunbathed. I have heard that the falls are beautiful with gold, red, and orange leaves and that winter is gorgeous as well with snow-capped trees. I also love the old architecture of the red brick buildings.

Of course I would not spend all of my time gazing at the trees and watching street performers in Harvard Square. Harvard also offers so many interesting courses. The Freshman Expository Writing course sounds difficult yet intriguing. I would love to take the macroeconomics course, the introduction to psychology course, and the history course on China. Looking through the course catalog, I think that there are more courses that I would like to take than I could ever possibly fit in my four year schedule.

Outside of academics, Harvard offers such a variety of extracurricular activities as well. I would love to volunteer with a public service organization. I would also like to star in one of the student theater productions and maybe even play intramural soccer.

My dream has always been to go to Harvard. The student body is so diverse and talented. The activities are innumerable, and the academic requirements are rigorous. The environment is truly indescribable. I know I would be a good addition to the next entering freshman class.

Comments On "Harvard Is Perfect For Me"

Missy's essay is little more than a simplified regurgitation of Harvard's glossy brochure. Does she really need to tell an admissions officer who has been working for years at Harvard that nearby Boston is a "historical city?" Would he or she even care? Missy lists a lot of information about what the reader already knows—

the college–and little information about what they know nothing–
her. This essay says very little about the author except that she
can read an information packet and course book.

Greed Is Good
● ● ● ● ● ● ● ●

By: Tony A.

My greatest hero is Gordon Gecko. In the movie "Wall Street," Gecko,
played by Michael Douglas, gave the most inspiring speech ever, his
"Greed is good" speech. There is no other phrase that so accurately
represents my goal in life. Some in this world may want to work to
feed the hungry, enter the realm of politics, or travel around the world.
But my sole goal in life is to earn as much money as I can. Of course, I
do not want money just so that I can buy things for myself. Once I
accumulate enough money, I will donate at least 10 percent of it to
charities such as the United Way and homeless shelters. I am a firm
believer in philanthropy.

My college education will be the first step toward attaining this
goal. I will study business during my four years. After graduating, I
will work for a financial institution in investment banking. While I
know that my hours will be rigorous, it will be worth the time. After
spending two years in investment banking working for a prestigious
firm, I will enter one of the top five business schools in the country.
After that, I will start my own financial institution. I want my company
to be worth millions within three years, and I want my salary to be
either six or seven digits. This way, I will be a millionaire before my
30th birthday.

I have been told that I have a one-track mind, and I guess that I
would agree. I do see almost everything in terms of profits and losses.
However, I think that I am justified. I think that I can best help improve
the world by earning as much money as I can. Once I earn enough
money, I will donate a tax-deductible percentage to charities. If I didn't
have that money in the first place, I wouldn't be able to donate it. By
attending your college, I will be well on my way toward achieving
this goal.

Comments On "Greed Is Good"

It would have helped if Tony had the money now. At least he could have offered a large donation to the college, although even then we doubt that it would have made any difference. We have told you not to write about how much money you have now or how much money you want to have in the future. This is one of the admissions officers' greatest turn-offs and now you see why. Colleges don't want to be flooded with heartless, egocentric money-mongers whose sole focus is on their own well-being. Colleges want good people who will contribute in positive ways.

Education Is The Key To Success
• • • • • • • • • • • • • • • • • • • •

By: Chuck C.

To me the pursuit of education has always been of the highest importance. Ever since I was a little boy, my father and mother told me, "Chuckie, education is the most important thing in life. It is the key to your future." In my youthful ignorance at the time, I was skeptical and did not believe them. However, today I know the truth of my parents' words of wisdom imparted to me so long ago.

Throughout school I have always given 100%. I have elected to take difficult classes when I could have taken easy ones. I have always completed my homework. I have always studied hard for every test. My hard work has paid off—I've earned all "A's" and "B's" in high school. This has made my parents proud. They say to me, "Chuck, we are so proud of you. Education really is the key to success."

When I say the pursuit of education is important, I am taking into account that in this world there is a lot to learn. We can learn about nature, science, cultures, mathematics, and history to name a few subjects. I think that every person should try to learn as much as possible about as many things as possible.

For example, I want to learn as much as I can about other cultures. By doing this, I can expand my knowledge of the world. I can cross racial, ethnic, and cultural boundaries. I also want to learn about nature. I want to appreciate the beauty of the outdoors and learn about animals, plants, and our environment. I also want to learn about history. I think history teaches us lessons about the past that are very important to our future.

In this way, education is the most important thing in life. Education expands our minds. It exposes us to new information. It takes us to a higher level. Education makes people better. It provides them with knowledge about the world, nature, and other people. It exposes them to new ideas and new thoughts. It is what places us at the top of the evolutionary chain. These are the reasons why education is so important in life. This is my purpose for going to college. I want to become truly educated. I want to raise my mind to a higher level, to be exposed to new ideas, and to learn as much as I possibly can.

Comments On "Education Is The Key To Success"

In this essay, Chuck writes about the merits of higher education, an appropriate topic, but one that he treats too generally. All students who apply to college are implicitly making the same statement—that they value education. Otherwise, they wouldn't bother to apply, right? Chuck should have explained why education is significant to him as an individual, what specifically he wants to learn more about, and why certain topics excite his intellect more than others. He should have focused on specific experiences rather than ramble about general principles.

When comparing many of these essays that failed to the essays that were successful, you probably have noticed that one consistent difference is that the essays that worked were all very specific in focus and did not try to say everything about a topic. So, keep your focus narrow and make every sentence you write interesting.

We Can Learn A Lot From The Japanese
• •

By: Angela L.

Last summer I traveled out of the country for the first time. I spent the summer in Japan living with a host family as an exchange student. Even though my stay was a short three months, I still learned a lot about the Japanese way of life. While both the United States and Japan are advanced countries and have some commonalities, I discovered many differences between our two nations.

The Japanese people have such a rich culture that is shared among everyone. In America, of course, we have little culture that is shared by everyone. There are so many people with such diverse backgrounds. We celebrate Christmas, Hanukkah, and the Winter Solstice, to name a few American winter holidays. Each of these holidays has an entirely different background and way of being celebrated. In Japan, however, everyone celebrates the same holidays. Even though we have more diversity in America, there is something special about knowing that on a given day nearly every person in the country is celebrating in a similar way. There is something harmonious about such unity.

The Japanese also have a different way of life. For example, they remove their shoes before entering their homes to keep their straw mat floors clean. They oftentimes sleep on futons on the floor that they fold up and tuck away in the morning. They eat with chopsticks, and their diet mainstays are white rice, a variety of noodles, and vegetables. On the other hand, we usually wear our shoes inside carelessly tracking in mud and dirt. We sleep in beds that we do not have to move in order to make needed space. We oftentimes eat meals made up of the McDonald's or Pizza Hut food group.

In our countries, we also have different work ethics. Japanese businessmen leave their homes before the sun rises to commute an hour to two hours to their offices. They spend much of their lives there because work is everything. When they socialize, it is usually with their business partners. In flocks, they head to bars for late night drinks and business talks. They vacation with their co-workers, too. Much of their lives revolves around their work. In America, work is also an integral part of life, but for most Americans it is not the only part. American workers enjoy socializing with their friends from outside of the company as well. Americans also enjoy vacationing with their families. For most American people, their lives do not revolve around work as is oftentimes true for Japanese businessmen.

Another difference between America and Japan is the educational system. Japan's educational system is based on examinations. After every level of school—elementary, junior high, and high school—students take an examination. The results of these examinations determine the quality of school which the students may attend. Within this system, students oftentimes as young as elementary school spend months and even years in advance preparing for the exams. They know that their test scores will determine not only what schools they are accepted to but eventually what level job they will hold and what incomes they will receive. While many students in the United States try to do well, this kind of pressure on students as early as elementary school does not exist.

Thus, after living in Japan last summer, I came to realize that there are many differences between the two countries. There is much that each could learn from exposure to the other.

Comments On "We Can Learn A Lot From The Japanese"

Although Angela's essay is marginally interesting if you have never been to Japan, it still failed to get her into a top college. The reason: Angela's essay says little about Angela. She has written an essay that sounds like it came from a tour book. Instead of reporting the differences in a provocative and enlightening way, Angela merely catalogs the contrasts. How much more interesting would it have been had she engaged the reader with a comparison of her host mother's life with her own mother's life? Angela tries to cover too much and ends up with an essay that is totally boring. It is impossible to write about all of the differences between two cultures in the limited space of a college essay. She would have had a much better essay if she had focused on a single difference. Angela's generic introduction and point by point structure leave nothing to the imagination. No memorable examples are given or vivid images created. This is an eminently forgettable essay.

Power Of Poetry
• • • • • • • • •

By: Henry L.

If poetry be the wine then I the drunkard. If poetry be the rifle then I the marksman. Nothing has so profoundly altered my mortal existence than the discovery of the poetic word.

Poetry offers such penetration into the human condition with a passion and propensity that is unmatched by any other endeavour since it has the ability to capture the essence of the emotional spirit and combine it with discursive attributes which stimulate our acknowledgment of the human condition and privilege our understanding of our innate value vis a vis the syndrome of mortality.

My own work in the construction, deconstruction, and reconstruction of the poetic has blossomed from a fleeting fascination with rhythm and rhyme to an intense desire to hone my sense of utterance so that it is neither myopic in its treatment of the sensual predications of modern existence nor ignorant to the monster of nativism. I hope that my constructs do not descend into the ephemeral but solidify as monumental testaments to the intellect of man and his thorough understanding of what can only be called the "floating world."

If offered admission into your school I will employ my time and energy into further developing my talents to effect an impact which would have repercussions throughout our metaphysical conception of being. It is to this mission and the leveraging of poetry which I dedicate my existence and consider my sacrament.

Comments On "Power Of Poetry"

Too bad no one can understand this essay. We doubt even Henry could explain exactly what he meant to say. Notice the ridiculously long sentences and hyperbolic words that add confusion rather than clarity. Nothing will hurt your chances more than an unintelligible essay. While admissions officers are a well-educated bunch, do not assume that they will be able to understand your thoughts unless you can explain them clearly.

A Final Note On The Essays That Bombed

It should be obvious that one major problem with the last seven essays is that the students did not spend enough time developing their ideas and crafting their sentences. In all likelihood none were edited by anyone other than the writer. All of these essays could have been winners if the students had spent more time, followed the suggestions in Chapter 5, and found editors to read their work. No essay is ever perfect the first time it is written. It takes a lot of rewriting and editing to make it a winning college essay. These essays bombed because they were first drafts submitted as final copy.

Do yourself a favor and get an early start. Don't worry about what your essay looks like after you write the initial draft. Keep working. Get someone to look it over and make suggestions. Re-read Chapter 5. The only essay that counts is the one you ultimately turn in to the admissions office.

Do You Have A Few Good Essays?

We are always looking for examples of college essays. If you have an essay that helped you get into a good school, why not send it to us? If we use it in our next book, we will give you full credit and even pay for the rights to print it. Hey, the essay got you into college why not let it help you pay for college, too! You can mail your essays to:

Jim Good and Lisa Lee
c/o 101 Publishing
4546 B10 El Camino Real, Suite 281
Los Altos, California 94022

THE SECRETS OF
THE INTERVIEW

In This Chapter
- ▲ Stories From Real Life: Why The Interview Doesn't Count
- ▲ How To Have The Most Intriguing Conversations Ever
- ▲ What Homework You Need To Do Before The Interview
- ▲ Why You Should Leave The Halter Top & Shorts Behind
- ▲ Nail Polish, Aspirin, & Other Emergency Supplies
- ▲ How To Prep For The Real Thing
- ▲ Why Blowing It Isn't Blowing It

The Interview Nightmare

Your essays may take more time to write and your grades more effort to earn, but for many students there is nothing more nerve-racking, stomach-churning, and downright intimidating than the college interview. Unlike the rest of your application, which will be evaluated in the private offices of the admissions officers, the interview will put you face to face with an actual person who appears to have the almighty power to get you in or keep you out of the school of your dreams.

Before you consider forging a letter from your doctor saying that your health prohibits you from taking part in live conversations, take some time to read this chapter. In it you will discover numerous things that you can do to prepare yourself for the interview and to make it more of a friendly chat than an interrogation.

Plus, if this promise is not enough of an assurance, we'll let you in on a little secret that the colleges definitely do not want you to know: the interview is really not that important. Are you surprised? Read on.

Why The Interview Does Not Matter

My interview for a well-known Ivy League college was relatively stress free. My interviewer was very nice and seemed more interested in answering my questions about student life than pounding me with tough questions about my academic performance or interests. In fact, by the end of the interview, I felt as if I had already been accepted and my interviewer was trying to convince me to choose his school over other rival colleges.

A few months later I got an acceptance letter from this school. After accepting their offer of admission, I called my interviewer to inform him of my decision and to thank him for the interview. We ended up having lunch together where I heard more praise for my decision.

Near the end of our lunch, I innocently asked my interviewer how important the interview had been and if it may have made the difference in my acceptance. My interviewer looked around as if to see if anyone was eavesdropping on our conversation. He took a sip of coffee and told me the little-known secret about the real role of the interview. He said that when he received his assignments of people to interview, the list separated the applicants into three categories: those who the admissions officers strongly wanted to admit, those who they strongly wanted to reject, and those who fell in the middle.

Before my interview took place, he knew that I had a good chance of getting accepted. In fact, he admitted that he had been so worried that I might accept an offer from another school that he felt he had to push the college as much as possible.

This explained why I felt my interview was more like a sales pitch. I wish I had known this before the interview. It would have saved me from some unnecessary butterflies.

By: Robert J. who still keeps in touch with his interviewer, now friend.

In the grand scheme of the application process, the interview is one of the least important parts. In fact, many schools use the interview not as a major determinant of admissions but rather as a check in the process. Usually the colleges will already have enough information to decide whether to admit you or not.

There are cases, however, when an applicant who looked good on paper turned out to be a total dimwit in person. Weeding out these few deceptive applicants is the interview's main job. If colleges get reports back from an interviewer saying that the applicant showed up in a T-shirt and shorts and had trouble composing a coherent sentence, they will certainly think twice about offering admission regardless of how stellar that student's application.

Although the main role of the interview is to confirm the preliminary decisions of the admissions board, it is of course still a good idea to prepare for the interview. If you are in the borderline group, your interview may be that extra something that pushes you into the admit group.

If an interviewer is particularly impressed by one of the borderline students, he or she will write a strong letter of support. Admissions officers have been known on a few occasions to change their mind based on an interviewer's passionate appeal. While this is not typical, it is still a possibility.

Secrets Of The Interview

Now that you know the interview is not as important as you thought, you may be able to relax a little. No amount of reassurance (and even practice for that matter) will totally eliminate the stress of the actual interview. However, if you adhere to the following advice we guarantee that you will not only possess a much higher level of confidence, but you will also make a strong, positive impression that could cement your acceptance to the school.

Make The Most Of Your Sweaty Palms

Not that this will provide you with solace, but with nerves on edge and not knowing exactly what to expect, your first interview will probably seem like a total disaster. Many of the questions will be unexpected and some may even stump you. This, however awful it may seem, is normal.

Your last interview, by contrast, will probably be your best. An experienced veteran, you will no longer be as nervous, you will be able to anticipate what questions your interviewer will ask, and you will have developed a repertoire of answers that you can apply to almost any question.

Thus, you should take advantage of the fact that your palms will become less sweaty as you do more interviews by scheduling your interviews strategically. Arrange to have your second- or third-choice school interviews first, and save your first-choice schools for last. By arranging to have your least important interviews first you will minimize the impact of your early interview nervousness while gaining confidence and experience to perform better in the interviews that really count.

Interviewers Are Real People Too

Remember when we were in elementary school, and we thought that our teachers were somehow above ordinary adults, that their sole purpose in life was to educate and discipline us, and that 24 hours a day they were at school doing who-knows-what kind of alien teacher rituals? Perhaps you still remember like we do the moment of revelation when you suddenly realized that your teachers actually had lives outside of school.

It is easy to view college interviewers, like our elementary school teachers, as something more than human. What you must realize is that interviewers, no matter which college they represent, are real people with real lives. Many interviewers are alumni who have volunteered through their alumni club to conduct the interviews; they are not high-ranking college officials.

Keep reminding yourself that the interviewer sitting across from you is an ordinary human being since this will help you to relax and view your interviewer in the right context. Think of him or her as a good adult friend or relative. If you can view your interviewer as a real person who enjoys interesting conversations, you will be able to establish an easy rapport, which will help make your interview both pleasant and memorable.

Going in too stiff and intent only on reciting your accomplishments and your memorized list of the benefits of going to college is a sure recipe for disaster. As the next strategy explains, you should try to engage in dynamic conversation rather than stiff Q&A.

Don't Just Talk About You

Since the interviewers are real people, they value real conversations. What would you prefer: listening to a one-hour soliloquy, with Socratic references, on the merits of academia as perceived through the eyes of an 18-year-old or participating in an intriguing conversation about current events, life experiences, and personal opinions? Needless to say, most interviewers prefer the latter.

Throughout your interviews, remind yourself that your goal is to achieve two-way conversation. Be careful of any interview where the subject is *you* and *you* dominate the interview talking about *your* accomplishments. Don't worry about trying to mention all of your achievements–your interviewer will ask about them. At the same time, however, this is not the only thing the interview is about.

Common sense tells us that most people enjoy talking about themselves, and interviewers are no different. Your interviewers volunteered for this job because they enjoyed their college experience and they like talking to potential students. Interviewers are usually the kind of people who love to give advice to young prospects. Think of this as a time not only for your interviewers to learn about you but for you to find out as much as you can about them and their experiences.

Creative Digressions And Connecting: How To Become Bosom Buddies With Your Interviewers

The more you know about your interviewers the better. At the beginning of the interview after greetings are exchanged, take a few moments to get to know your interviewers. Ask them about their current profession, their college major, and where they were born and raised. Be friendly but don't be ingratiating.

Another big hint for the interview: Look on their walls. The first thing you should do when you walk into the interviewer's office is search your surroundings for clues. Clues can be anything: a diploma on the wall, picture of your interviewer receiving an award from IBM, Museum of Fine Arts calendar, or a Mr. Potato Head on the desk. Clues are invaluable sources about who you are meeting, what they enjoy, and what makes them proud.

Throughout the interview, ask your interviewers questions about themselves and their experiences during and after college. Of course, do not go overboard by barraging them with an unending stream of questions, but make sure that the conversation is engaging for them as well.

For example, let's say that your interviewer asks you what you enjoy most about school and you respond with the math team. If while you are answering the question, the interviewer makes some remark like, "Oh, I enjoyed that too" or "Yes, I understand it was like that for me also" or any other comment that indicates you have something in common, take advantage of it. Ask your interviewer a follow-up question. "Were you in your school's math club?" or "What do you think about Berkeley's math department?" may spark an interesting two-way conversation with your interviewer and you may even discover that you have some mutual interests.

You should not follow every question your interviewer asks with your own question, but when the opportunity presents itself, take it. Again, the goal is to try to engage your interviewer in a two-way, dynamic dialogue.

Listen, Too

It really is true that the best conversationalists are also the best listeners. If you happen to get interviewers (and the chances are high) who really love to talk, let them. One student told us that in his Princeton interview his interviewer spoke 90% of the time. He thought that the interview had been a total disaster since he hardly

How I Got In By Jabbering About Karate

A friend of ours named Rob used to brag that he got into Cornell simply by acing his interview. From the very first question Rob said he hit it off with his interviewer, with whom he shared a passion for karate. Two hours of two-way conversation sped by without either person noticing.

Rob's claim that he got into Cornell simply by bonding with his interviewer is highly questionable—in addition to a dynamite interview, he also had remarkable grades and held several leadership positions. Still, his experience certainly shows how connecting with interviewers can make the time much more enjoyable and provide you with strong support from them. This can make a difference if you're a borderline candidate.—Authors

Before my interview my college guidance counselor advised me to have a list of possible topics to speak about including such fascinating things as current events, my favorite book, and a philosophical debate. When I arrived at the law office of Jill Stevens and saw the pictures of her in a karate uniform on the wall, I knew our conversation would take a different turn.

Jill's first question was about my interests, and I immediately seized on the opportunity to talk about my involvement with karate at school and the local YMCA. I learned that Jill had been taking karate lessons for just over a year and was very interested in progressing through the ranks. She asked me question after question about my technique, training, and instructor. We had a great conversation about the benefits of karate in disciplining the mind and improving concentration. I commended her on her achievement in such a short time and even recommended a dojo where her 5-year-old son could try karate.

Instead of the usual stuff about my academic achievements and interests in school, we spent two hours talking about our mutual love of karate. It worked out for me. I was accepted by the school with, as Jill later told me, an enthusiastic letter of support from her. Plus, I really didn't want to talk about current events anyway.

By: Rob J. who is now a volunteer interviewer himself.

got a chance to speak about himself and his accomplishments. This applicant was very surprised when at the end of the interview his interviewer shook his hand and said very sincerely, "This was one of the best conversations I have had all week. Thank you."

Although the applicant's interviewer did all of the talking, from the interviewer's point of view since the applicant had been a good listener and had asked a few appropriate questions from time to time, the conversation was great. Had this student tried to wrest control of the interview, the interviewer would have felt like the student was uninterested or even pushy and rude. So, keep in mind that the goal of the interview is to establish a good two-way conversation. The worst thing you can do in an interview is do all the talking.

What Homework You Need To Do

Remember those college brochures filled with pictures, statistics, and text cultivating dust balls under your bed? Dig them out before your interview and do something terribly, horrifyingly radical—read them! It is not necessary to read them cover to cover, but knowing such basic facts as where the school is located, what kind of environment it has, some of the courses it offers, and some of the activities you may choose to participate in is a good idea. Needless to say it does not impress interviewers when they discover that students who are applying to their beloved alma mater do not even know what state it is located in or that the college is single sex. (There was an applicant who actually made it to the interview before he learned that the exclusive college he was applying to was an all-women school!)

If you can, try to talk to relatives or friends who now attend or have attended the college. They can give you insights into the college that are not found in the glossy brochures. The more you know the better.

Doing your homework will allow you to be able to ask intelligent questions when your interviewers ask you if you have any. You are making the most important decision in your life so far. It makes sense that you would have a question or two about it. Having prepared questions not only helps create the two-way conversation dynamic, but it also demonstrates that you are serious about attending the college.

Not all questions are good questions, and in particular, avoid asking those obvious questions whose answers are on the first page of the glossy brochures. Instead, the best questions to ask your interviewers are those that make them reflect on their own experience, require them to do a little thinking, and elicit an opinion. Making your interviewers think or express their opinions makes the interviews much more interesting for them and makes your question seem insightful and probing. Some examples:

▶ What do you think about the X department?

▶ How did the small/large class size affect your education?

▶ Did you have a lot of contact with your professors?

▶ What was the best opportunity you felt X university provided you?

▶ What is the best/worst aspect of X university or X city?

Think of some more and write them on a list with the most interesting ones at the top. Take this list into the interviews and refer to them when the conversation begins to stall and when your interviewers ask you if you have any questions.

Cheat Sheet Of The Most Commonly Asked Questions

In addition to doing your homework on the school, you need to do homework on yourself. In other words, you need to know how to speak about yourself intelligently and coherently. The best way to do this is to get a preview of what your interviewers will ask before the big event.

Throughout the history of interviewing, some interviewers have been known to pitch a couple of curve balls. Some unpleasant ones we've heard include: "Please estimate right now how many quarters it would take to build a column as tall as the Empire State building;" "Give us three convincing reasons for *not* admitting you;" and "I want you to do this interview without using the word 'I.'"

Fortunately, however, most interviewers choose from your standard fare of non-lethal questions. The following is a list of the most common questions that you should be prepared to answer. You can use these questions for your mock interviews, which are discussed later in this chapter.

▶ Why do you want to attend X university?

▶ What is your strongest/weakest point?

▶ What have you done to prepare for college?

▶ What has been your greatest experience in high school?

▶ What do you want to do in the future?

▶ Tell me about yourself. (You should focus on about three things.)

▶ Tell me about your interests.

▶ Tell me about your involvement in extracurricular activities.

▶ Tell me about your family.

▶ What do you think about [insert a current event of the past week]?

▶ What is your favorite book? Who is your favorite author?

▶ Which of your accomplishments are you the most proud of?

▶ If you could meet any important figure in the past or present, who would it be and what would you talk about?

▶ If you could be any animal what would you be? Why?

The "No-No" Topics

It may be pretty obvious to you that your college interview is not the best place to share your addiction to inhaling paint thinner or that you have a collection of traffic tickets from all 50 states. However, some students have done exactly this.

As stated earlier, you should ask plenty of questions yourself to find something in common with your interviewers. Still, although your goal is to connect with your interviewers, there are, of course, some topics that you should not bring up. While these topics may seem self-evident to you, they are topics that students have actually brought up in their interviews. The "no-no" topics include:

▶ Your membership in a cult or any strong religious beliefs.

▶ How you want to single handedly instill world peace or end hunger or any other dream that would be viewed as unrealistic or overly idealistic.

▶ Your membership in the Anarchy of America Association or any other very radical or conservative political beliefs.

▶ Your passion for vodka or any other personal drug use.

▶ How you drove the getaway car in a bank holdup or any other less serious infraction of the law.

▶ Sex and your personal sexual history or experience.

▶ Why your parents think they are the King and Queen of England or any other sort of severe family dysfunction.

Of course you will have to be the ultimate judge of your interviewers and of what is an appropriate topic. If you have very strong religious beliefs, and you see that there are numerous religious icons in your interviewer's office, or if you are applying to a religious institution, then do talk about your dedication to the church. If your interviewer seems turned off by a shift in the conversation, change the topic as soon as possible. Throughout your interviews, take note of your interviewers' reactions to the topics you discuss.

Know The World Around You

If you are already knowledgeable about current events around the world, you will be very well prepared for the interview. If not, start reading the newspaper as frequently as possible so that you will have a basic knowledge of current events and issues.

Many interviewers ask all candidates a basic question on current events. They do not expect you to be an expert on the current political, economic, and social upheavals of the world, but they do want to know if you occasionally pick up a newspaper. Interviewers also want to see how you analyze issues such as, for example, a heated political election. It is difficult to demonstrate your analytical skills if you do not have the basic facts.

If you are surprised with a question that you know nothing about, you should admit your lack of knowledge and try to give as much information as possible about what you do know. It is better to admit your lack of knowledge than risk making a total fool out of yourself by acting like you know what you are talking about when you clearly do not.

You may also want to keep extremely conservative, liberal, or radical views to yourself. While your idea to cure the world's ills through a global day of nakedness may be revolutionary, you probably do not want to make such a view public—at least not yet. You want to show your interviewers your thoughtful and opinionated side, not your lunatic fringe side.

As your interviewers are "normal" people, they too have opinions. If yours are the polar opposites of theirs and you engage in debate, they may appreciate you for expressing your opinions, but they may also dislike you for disagreeing with them. Once you enter the college of your dreams you can take center stage and extol any and all opinions (including your proposed day of nakedness). Before then, however, our advice is to keep any extreme opinions to yourself.

No Snoozing Allowed

A simple mistake that many students make during their interviews is simply not showing interest in what their interviewers have to say. Throughout your conversation with your interviewers, always appear as interested as you can. Ask questions. Respond to what they say. Take a notebook and a pen to write down any information your interviewers provide. This will visibly show them that you value their opinions and that you are serious about your desire to attend their alma mater. If you start to feel sleepy, start taking notes on your conversation or ask for a second cup of coffee. The best cure for a sudden attack of drowsiness is to keep the conversation lively and interesting.

The Mock Interview

The best way to prepare for the interviews is to do them. If your school offers mock interviews be sure to take advantage of them. If not, ask a friend or family member to act as an interviewer and do a mock interview at home. If you cannot find someone who will play interviewer, you can play the part yourself by asking and then answering your own questions. (Warning: If you do this in public people *will* think that you are crazy.)

To make the mock interview a real learning experience you should try to videotape or tape record it. Use the questions provided in this chapter as well as any others that you think might be asked. Find a quiet place with two chairs. Sit face to face with your interviewer and go for it.

Try as much as possible to act like you are at a real interview. Practice creating two-way conversation, talking about meaningful topics, and expressing your opinions. You can even instruct your interviewer to purposefully create dead time where he or she does not say anything so you can practice jump starting the conversation with a question or comment.

When you are finished, ask your interviewer for his or her opinion. Did you speak clearly and slowly enough? Was the conversation interesting? Were the topics you chose appropriate? Did your personality come across well? Ask for suggestions for improvement, and be sure to treat them as constructive criticisms.

Review the tape and try to locate weak areas. Did a question throw you off? Re-work your answers in your head or on paper and try the interview again. Doing as many mock interviews as possible with as many interviewers as you can find will greatly reduce the stress and improve your performance for the real thing.

During one of your mock interviews make sure that you wear your actual interview clothes. You may find that the collar of your favorite shirt is just a little too tight to speak comfortably for an extended period. Check to make sure that your slacks, dress, or skirt feels comfortable when you sit.

Leave The Halter Top And Shorts Behind

Speaking of clothes—they do a lot in establishing a first impression. Since your appearance will provide your interviewers with their first impression of you, you need to dress appropriately. This means leaving the sexy cut-off T-shirt that reveals your pierced belly button, super baggy jeans 40 sizes too large, and the mini-mini-mini patent leather skirt in the closet.

For men, dressing your part means a dress shirt, tie, and nice sports coat at a minimum. Even better however is a business suit. For women, a dress, dressy pants and blouse, or dressy skirt and blouse. We hear your groans, but by dressing well, you will appear professional and mature, which will be remembered when it comes time for your interviewers to evaluate you. If you are not sure about a particular outfit, it is better not to wear it.

More important than what you actually choose to wear, however, is that you wear what makes you feel most comfortable. You could be wearing a design straight from the pages of the latest fashion magazine, but if it does not fit well, your squirming and uneasiness will do more damage than if you had worn a simple hand-me-down suit from your older brother.

At least a day before your interview, put on your most comfortable outfits and make sure they are stain and wrinkle free. If you cannot choose between two outfits, go with the more conservative one. Don't forget to make sure that your footwear is clean and polished. Before your interviews, examine yourself in a mirror to check for any runs, rips, or other grooming faux pas.

Know How To Get Where You Are Going

You might think this is common sense, but be sure you know how to get to your interview. Invest in a map and take a test drive to the area if you are still unsure about the roads. Be sure to ac-

My Fishnet Stockings Spelled Rejection

The following is a hard to believe but true story. The student admits it is the truth but is, understandably, very embarrassed and cannot imagine that she was ever so naive. In order to protect her identity (and pride) she has assumed the pseudonym Helen.—Authors

I had heard from a friend that with the hundreds or even thousands of applicants admissions officers meet each year, it was best to wear clothes that stood out so that the interviewer would remember you most. This made sense, I thought. I definitely wanted to be remembered by the admissions officer, so I selected the flashiest getup in my closet, believing that the flashier the outfit, the more likely I would be remembered.

Decked out in a hot red satin top, black leather skirt, fishnet stockings, and thigh high boots, I entered the admissions office. I ignored the stares of the other students, dressed in suits and loafers, and took their surprise as evidence that my outfit would certainly be remembered.

When it was my turn, I walked confidently into the interviewer's office. I was prepared to explain how I was a leader at my school and how I was eager to begin college when the admissions officer stopped my train of thought. With her arms crossed and her eyes narrowed at me glaringly she snorted, "Do you think this is a night club, dear? Please come back again when you are dressed appropriately for a college interview." I was so embarrassed from her reaction that I never even went back for my interview, which probably sealed my rejection to the school.

For my next interview, I learned my lesson. Wearing a simple skirt and blouse sans the fishnet stockings, I was actually given the chance to complete my interview.

Note: Although Helen's outfit blew her first interview, she learned her lesson early. For the rest of her interviews, she dressed appropriately and was rewarded with an acceptance from Berkeley.

count for unpredictable road conditions such as construction and 50 car pile-ups. Leave your house with plenty of time to spare. If you arrive early, you can take a short walk to calm yourself down or review what you plan to say. In any case, you do not want the first impression you make to be that of tardiness.

Nail Polish, Aspirin, And Other Emergency Supplies

By emergency supplies, we do not mean a first aid kit or canned goods in case of an earthquake (although in certain areas of the country that would not be such a bad idea). What we are referring to is all of the supplies you may need in case of a mini-emergency such as a snag in your pantyhose or a sudden pang of nausea. Pack in your car, purse, or briefcase anything you think you could reasonably need in case of a mishap. For example: sewing kit, aspirin, stomach medicine, mouthwash, hairbrush, cosmetics, extra pantyhose, mirror, candy bar.

Remember that Murphy's Law will be in effect and what you least want or expect to happen, will. With these supplies, at least you will be prepared. Be sure to take a quick look at yourself in a mirror before you walk in and check to see that your hair is combed, tie straight, zipper up, and a piece of today's lunch is not still between your teeth.

Show Time! Psyche Yourself Up For The Real Thing

When it comes time for the Big Event, the most important thing to remember is to be yourself. When you are yourself, you are the most comfortable, the most natural, and the most likable. Interviewers can often detect when you are faking it by trying to be someone who you are not.

Remind yourself that your interviewers are real people and that you are going to have real conversations with these real people about your and their real lives. Try to think of this as a wonderful chance to meet interesting people and learn a little more about the colleges. And do not forget that while you want to put on your best performance, world peace does not hang in the balance. So, relax!

Why Blowing It Is Not Blowing It

If after your interview, you feel that you did not do as well as you wanted to, you are not the only one. Everyone has doubts after their interviews, especially the first one, and regrets not having asked a particular question or made such and such an insightful comment. All of this is apparent only after the interview is over. (Of course!)

As you replay the interview in your head, all kinds of clever responses that you could have made will come to mind, and your few mistakes and stumbles will appear glaringly large. This is perfectly normal. Fortunately, unlike you, your interviewers were not placing your every gesture and word under a microscope. While you may remember that you accidentally ended a sentence with a preposition, your interviewers will not.

Interviewers are looking not for the details but for an overall impression of you. If you engaged in two-way conversation, connected with them, and followed the other suggestions outlined in this chapter; you will have made a good impression. But since nothing will keep you from thinking about what you should have done, take advantage of this, and try to remember some of your better ideas. You may have an opportunity to use them in your next interview.

Finish With A Thank You

As you will recall, your interviewers are often volunteers, and volunteers love to feel appreciated. Make your interviewers feel this way by taking five minutes to write each of them a thank you note. Try to do this within a day so you can mail your letter soon after your interview. Not only will you come across as mature and well-mannered, but you will also create a final positive impression of yourself. When it comes time to report back to the admissions committee, your thanked interviewers will not forget your kind gesture.

PUT ON THOSE
FINISHING TOUCHES

●●●●●●●●●●●●●●●●●●●●●●●●●●●●●●●●●●

In This Chapter
▲ A Once, Twice, & Thrice Over
▲ The Most Important Dimes You'll Ever Spend
▲ The Big Send-Off
▲ Stories From Real Life: I Missed the Deadline By Four Days!
▲ The Big Dilemma: To Express, Prioritize, Or Register

You Are Done! (Well Almost...)

Congratulations! You have survived the most difficult part of the college admissions process. You have written a spectacular essay, filled out every blank on the application form, and had glowing reviews of yourself written by teachers and others. Whew! What an accomplishment. Before you start to party, there are still some easy, but nevertheless important, finishing touches you need to do before chucking that thick envelope into the mailbox.

Do A Once, Twice, & Thrice Over

At the risk of sounding like a nagging parent, you should check, double check, and even triple check to make sure that you have enclosed everything required for your applications. Forgetting something will not spell rejection, but it may slow down the admissions process. Here are some frequently overlooked items:

Application. Every blank and question should be completed. Also, most forms have an area at the top or on the side where you need to type your name.

Transcript. Forget about any schemes like whiting out less than perfect grades; colleges require an official copy. As a side note, one student recently attempted to white out all of the minuses on her report card. Suspecting foul play, the college requested an official transcript from the school. When the college confirmed the difference, the high school was informed, the student was punished, and she was promptly rejected from the college. It was a shame, especially since the minuses the student whited out belonged mostly to "A's" and she would have been a strong candidate with such a record.

Signatures. Yours, in all the right places. Especially on the application form certifying that what you have written is true.

Check. No free rides here. If you do not send the money, the colleges will not process your application.

Miscellaneous Envelopes, Postcards, Labels, Etc. To save money on processing, some schools have specific envelopes or postcards for correspondence that you address to yourself. Remember that times are tight for institutions of higher education and they often make you put on your own stamps.

Financial Aid Forms. These are usually due a few months later, but remember that every blank and question should be completed. Include tax forms and any other relevant forms. Take a look at Chapter 11 for more information on these special forms.

Also, do not forget to check:

Evaluations. Follow up with your teachers, counselors, and other recommenders to make sure that they submit your evaluations before the deadline.

Score Reports. Even if you'd rather keep them to yourself, don't forget to have the Educational Testing Services (ETS) and ACT Assessment send the reports for your SAT I, SAT II, ACT, APs and any other scores to the colleges.

Filing. If you apply to more than one college (and who does not) it is very easy to get things mixed up. Make sure you are sending the right essay to the right school, especially if all of your essays are similar. One student we know didn't check and discovered only after he had mailed his applications that he had accidentally sent all 14 schools the same essay in which he had declared his strongest desire to attend Duke!

The Most Important Dimes You'll Ever Spend

Before sending off the only existing copy of your completed application, splurge by spending a couple dimes to photocopy it. That way, if by some misfortune your application is lost in the mail or the school misplaces it, you will have a copy ready to send to them, and you will not have to go through the excruciating process of reconstructing your application. Also, when you are applying for scholarships or jobs in the future, you will find the information on the application forms to be very useful.

The Big Send-Off

Most college deadlines are based on the postmark. In other words as long as the postmark is on or before the due date, the application is considered to be on time. If you are the type who waits until the last possible moment to do anything, then you must gather every morsel of energy and self-discipline you have to combat this urge when mailing your applications. While we don't expect you to finish your applications six months before they are due–although that would certainly be nice–you should try to complete and mail your applications as early as possible. At the very least designate the day before they must be postmarked by as your deadline for mailing them.

Sure, you will miss the excitement of racing off to the post office at 4:59 and getting down on your knees to beg the postal worker to accept just one more letter, but you will insure that your application is received by the admissions office on time.

Having preached the virtue of finishing early and mailing on time, we must confess that sometimes application forms need to be mailed late. As you will see from the following Stories From Real Life, mailing your application past the deadline, while definitely not a smart move, does not necessarily mean instant rejection. But, we should warn you that even though the following story has a happy ending, we definitely do not recommend you try it!

I Missed The Deadline And Was Still Accepted

I promised myself again and again that this time I would not procrastinate, but nevertheless, I did. So on the night before three of my applications were due, I had an incredible amount of work left. I still had to add introductions to my essays as well as type all three of the application forms. I planned to go to sleep early and then wake up early to finish everything.

You can probably guess what happened. After I slept through my alarm and finally stumbled out of bed at 11 a.m., I still had so much to do that by the time 5 o'clock rolled around I realized that I was not going to be able to finish. It was a noble attempt, but I just was not fast enough. Rather than turn in a bad application, I decided to spend another day and express mail it. I ended up mailing all three applications several days late.

As I waited for the colleges to make their decisions, I had nightmares that the colleges would return my applications to me without even opening them. I began to wonder if I should write asking that my application fees be refunded. When the decision letters began to arrive, I cringed each time I approached the mailbox, expecting rejections from those three schools. To my amazement, I was accepted at all three schools and two even offered scholarships!

I was very lucky that things worked out. My advice is to do everything you can to prevent mailing an application late. If you absolutely, positively cannot finish an application by the deadline, I think it is better to mail it a few days late and take a chance than to submit an incomplete application or to not apply at all. However, you do risk being rejected without even being considered. Some colleges are more lenient than others, but you never can predict which ones will give you a break.

By: Emma G. who no longer procrastinates (too much) at Duke.

The Big Dilemma: To Express, Prioritize, Or Register

Every time you go to the post office you are faced with the most trying of dilemmas—choosing between the ever expanding service options of regular, express, priority, registered, certified, and more. While we are sure that there are reasons for offering such a variety, we'd like to see the post office simplify the choice by just offering three services: fast, faster, and fastest.

If you're mailing your applications before the deadline you can save some bucks by mailing them via regular airmail. If you have had trouble with lost packages you may want purchase a Certificate of Mailing. These are cheap—about 50 cents—and provide you with proof that you have sent your application. Colleges usually dislike it when students send their applications in one of the more fancy ways (such as registered) since this means that someone from the office must take time from their busy schedule to sign for the package.

The only time you will need to use express mail service is when you are mailing past the deadline. But, this shouldn't happen, right?

Thank All Of Your Helpers

Make Miss Manners proud by writing thank you letters to everyone who helped you along the way. Not only is it the polite thing to do, but it will also make those who have helped you feel appreciated and useful. Include letters to your teachers and other recommenders, interviewers, editors, advisors, and anyone else who deserves a thank you. Do not forget to also tell them where you have been accepted and where you have decided to attend.

If you feel like it go ahead and send us a letter telling us where you will be going to school and how our book may have helped you get there. We'd love to hear from you! Send your letters to:

Jim Good and Lisa Lee
c/o 101 Publishing
4546 B10 El Camino Real, Suite 281
Los Altos, California 94022

THE ALPHABET SOUP OF TESTS: HOW TO ACE THEM

In This Chapter

▲ How To Avoid SAT Hell
▲ Revealed: The Real Importance Of The SAT & ACT
▲ Over 50 Ways To Increase Your Scores By 100 Points
▲ A Timeline For Testing
▲ How To Deal With A Bombed Test

Avoid SAT Hell

One of the most detested aspects of applying to college is the fact that you will spend no less than six excruciating hours on early Saturday mornings taking a series of tedious tests that pit you against every other college-bound high school senior in the country. The results of this stressful experience will be a set of numbers that you can use to compare yourself to your friends to see who really is smarter! Of course, the worst part is that you will have to mail these scores to the colleges, which will use them to help decide if you are worthy of admission. It's no wonder that some students have been attending after-school test prep courses since they were in pre-school. But how important are these tests anyway?

You may find it hard to believe, but there was a time when students didn't worry about these tests. On the appointed day they got up, went to school, took the test, and that was it.

Those days are no more. Now, most students (and parents) unfortunately subscribe to the myth that these tests are the only things that count in college admissions. Just go to the bookstore and see how many books there are on how to master, crack, or outsmart these tests. Check out the yellow pages and see how many test prep schools and academic counselors are listed.

How this hype surrounding these tests has come to be, we do not know. But it sure is enough to scare any college bound senior. So, before you fall into this state of mind we call SAT Hell, let us try to clear up some of the misunderstandings.

MYTH #1: Standardized Tests Make Or Break Your Chances Of Admission.

Absolutely not true! While it is true that standardized tests are important in the admissions process, they are certainly not the only determinant of your admission into college. A friend of ours who scored 1560 on the SAT I was passed over by Harvard, while another friend who barely broke 1100 was accepted.

The reality is that admissions officers are interested in more than just the numbers. When they evaluate students' applications, they take into consideration all of the components including the application, evaluation letters, essay, academic record, awards, work experience, leadership and extracurricular activities, and (in borderline cases) the interview.

To think that test scores top all of these factors is simply wrong. In fact, between: a) your grades and the types of classes you took; and b) your SAT scores, the former is much more useful in predicting how successful you will be in college. Admissions officers know from experience that it is safer to accept an academically motivated but low testing student than the opposite.

MYTH #2: You Have To Score Over 1350 To Get Into Harvard Or Any Other Elite School.

As mentioned above, test scores will not doom you to rejection. Thus, when you are looking at the profiles of colleges in the guidebooks, don't get worked up because your scores are lower than a certain median or percentile.

Many guidebooks provide a median score for each school, which indicates the score at which half the students scored better and half scored worse. Some schools list ranges between which most of their students who are admitted scored. These numbers can give you a good target to aim for, but keep in mind that every year thousands of students with good high school records but lower than average test scores are admitted to top schools.

If your scores are lower than the scores in the guidebooks, remember that admissions officers do realize that even well-qualified and motivated students do not always perform well on standardized tests. A student with a high GPA but an average SAT score is just as competitive (if not more so) than someone with an average GPA but high SAT score. Plus, there are many other factors that admissions officers evaluate when making their decisions. Academic performance, teacher evaluations, and the essay can be much more important than any single test score.

In short: the scores count, but they are not the most important factor in admissions decisions. Don't take yourself out of the running if don't get a "high" score. Of course, try your best since it certainly won't hurt your chances to get the best score possible.

MYTH #3: There Is Nothing You Can Do To Prepare For These Tests.

All tests would be easier if we didn't have to study for them. Unfortunately, the standardized tests for college admissions are not these kinds of tests. To perform well, you must practice and study. Fortunately, there are several ways to study the material you will be tested on as well as to improve your test-taking skills. The tips given in this chapter will help you prepare for these tests effectively.

However, whichever method you choose to study for these tests do not spend so much time that your grades or participation in extracurricular activities suffers. If you devote so much time to studying at the expense of your grades and activities you will greatly hurt your chances of getting accepted. Be careful how much time you devote to test preparation.

Now that we have dispelled some of the myths that surround these tests, let's take a look at each test in more detail and see how you can improve your scores.

The Ingredients Of The Alphabet Soup Of Tests

Here are the ingredients of the alphabet soup of test: the SAT I, SAT II, ACT, PSAT, APs, and for non-native English speakers: the TOEFL, TWE, and TSE. In case you are not yet familiar with these tests, it's time to get acquainted. After all, you can't start studying for a test unless you know what will be on it. For more detailed information on the alphabet soup of tests and to register to take one, ask your counselor for the test information booklets written by the test makers or refer to Appendix A on where to write for copies.

The SAT I: Reasoning Test

The SAT I, the Scholastic Assessment Test (previously known as the Scholastic Aptitude Test), is perhaps the one with which you are the most familiar. It is the granddaddy of all the tests, the one to which the most preparatory manuals and courses are devoted and the one that often creates the most anxiety. The SAT I covers two general areas in three hours—math and verbal. Each is scored between 200 and 800 for a combined possible score of 1600.

The Math Section

Arithmetic, algebra, and geometry are tested. This sounds simple, but under the pressure of the clock and of competing against thousands of other students, it can be a challenge.

The key is to go into the exam with an intimate knowledge of the different types of questions. Later in this chapter, we will give you specific strategies on how to attack the math questions, but first here is a sample of each type of question:

Multiple Choice With Five Possible Answers. For example, JoJo, Junior, and Jiji got in a fight over x number of jelly beans. If JoJo ended up with three times as many jelly beans as Junior and if Jiji ended up with twice as many jelly beans as JoJo, how many jelly beans did Junior end up with, in relation to x?

(A) x/3   (B) x/5   (C) x/6   (D) x/10   (E) x/12

(*Answer*: JoJo had three times as many jelly beans as Junior. If Junior had n jelly beans, then JoJo had 3n jelly beans. JiJi had two times as many jelly beans as JoJo, which is 6n jelly beans. All of their jelly beans added together equal x, meaning n + 3n + 6n =x or 10n=x. We are trying to figure out how many jelly beans Junior had. Since he had n jelly beans, we could divide 10n=x by 10. This would result in n=x/10. Answer: D.)

Quantitative Comparison With Four Choices. For these questions you will compare two values to determine, if possible, which is greater or if they are equal. On your answer sheet you will choose:

A–if the quantity in Column A is greater.
B–if the quantity in Column B is greater.
C–if the two quantities are equal.
D–if the relationship can't be determined from the information given.

You should memorize these instructions so you don't waste time reading them during the actual test. An example might be:

Column A	Column B
p/2	p/3

(*Answer*: If p=1, then 1/2 is greater than 1/3, meaning that Column A is greater. However, if p=-1, then -1/2 is less than -1/3, meaning that Column B is greater. Therefore, we can't determine the answer from the information given. Answer: D.)

"Fill-in" Or "Student-Produced Response." You will provide your own answer to a question like: A poll was conducted at a high school with 1,000 students to see who the "super popular" kids were. The rules stated that the students must be first rated "popular" in order to be judged "super popular." If 30 percent of the students were rated "popular," and 70 percent of the "popular" students were voted "super popular," how many students were "super popular"?

(*Answer*: 1,000 students x .30 = 300 "popular" students. (300 x .70 = 210 "super popular" students. Answer: 210 students.)

That's it for the math section. Did you get the right answers? If not, it's time to pull out those old math books!

In keeping with today's shedding of human thought in favor of machines, ETS now lets you use a calculator on the SAT I Math Section. Don't start celebrating yet, thinking that your friend the calculator will do all the work for you. None of the problems on the exam can be solved with a simple click of a few keys; you have to invest some brain power as well. In fact, the SAT gurus recommend that you don't use your calculator on every problem. Some are still faster to solve the archaic pen and paper way.

The Verbal Section

The Verbal Section tests your ability to analyze reading passages, sentence structures, and connections between pairs of words. There are three kinds of questions:

Critical Reading. You will read passages and pairs of passages on such exciting topics as the history of coal mining and the mating habits of the Monarch butterfly. Following each passage or pair of passages are questions to test your comprehension.

Analogies. Your job in this section is to play matchmaker, picking out pairs of words that share the most similar relationship. Analogies test both your vocabulary and your ability to understand connections between words. Here's an example we devised based on the real test structure:

STRESS:PERSPIRE::
(A) eye:tear
(B) bacteria:mold
(C) ice:melt
(D) joy:melancholy
(E) cold:shiver

(*Answer:* Try to make a sentence that expresses the relationship of the analogy. Stress causes our bodies to perspire. Looking at the answer choices E best expresses this relationship. Answer: E.)

Sentence Completion. We like to call this part of the test the *Mad Libs* section. For each question, there is a sentence with one or two blanks. From five choices, you must pick the word or words that best fit into the blanks. Unlike *Mad Libs*, however, you want your sentences to make sense, not make your friends roll over laughing. The Sentence Completion questions test your vocabulary and language usage. For example:

Unable to make the final decision between Stanford and Harvard, Fred took the __ route of visiting the town __ to learn his destiny.

(A) unmistakable...fortuneteller
(B) unconventional...teacher
(C) unorthodox...soothsayer
(D) religious...priest
(E) extended...leader

(*Answer*: C.)

The trick to getting a high score on the SAT Verbal Section is to know a lot of vocabulary. Most of the sections require that you know the meaning of some very difficult words. So, the sooner you start to buff up your vocabulary the better!

The PSAT

Don't think that as a sophomore or junior you will miss out on all the fun of taking the alphabet soup of tests. You have the opportunity to take the PSAT (Preliminary Scholastic Assessment Test) as practice for the real thing. The format is the same as the SAT I although the test is shorter. You can take the PSAT at anytime during high school and you should check with your school to find out when it will be given. While your PSAT scores will not affect your admissions into college, your score from your junior year will be used to determine if you qualify for a National Merit Scholarship. If you do you will receive some money to help pay for tuition. This scholarship is based solely on merit. So whether for practice or to try to win a National Merit Scholarship, you should be sure to take the PSAT during your junior year.

The SAT II: Subject Tests

These exams consist of over 20 tests in 5 subject areas: English, Math, History, Science, and Language. Thankfully you don't have to take all of them. Individual schools may have different requirements for the tests, but most require that students take three exams. The SAT II tests, like the SAT I, are based on an 800-point scale. Each exam lasts for one hour. The Subject Tests are:

English
Literature
Writing

Mathematics
Mathematics Level I
Mathematics Level IC (calculator permitted)
Mathematics Level IIC (calculator permitted)

History
American History and Social Studies
World History

Sciences
Biology
Chemistry
Physics

Languages
Chinese with Listening
English Language Proficiency
French (reading only)
French with Listening
German (reading only)
German with Listening
Italian
Japanese with Listening
Korean with Listening
Latin
Modern Hebrew
Spanish (reading only)
Spanish with Listening

The ACT

There is one way you can sneak out of taking the SAT I. That is by taking another standardized test: the ACT. Most colleges accept either SAT or ACT scores. Administered by The American College Testing Program, the ACT lasts almost three hours and covers four subject areas: English, Math, Reading, and Science. You will receive a score for each of the 4 subject areas and a composite (average) score for the entire test between 1 and 36. Approximately half of the students tend to earn composite scores of about 20 or higher.

If you are going to take the ACT you will be faced with the following sections:

The English Test. You'd better bone up on your parts of speech and comma placement because this part of the ACT has multiple-choice questions covering two areas: English Mechanics (punctuation, grammar, and sentence structure) and Rhetorical Skills (organization and style).

The Math Test. This test has multiple-choice questions covering mathematics courses taken up until the beginning of the 12th grade: pre-algebra, elementary algebra, intermediate algebra, coordinate geometry, plane geometry, and trigonometry. Like the SAT, the ACT allows you to use a calculator.

The Reading Test. This test contains college freshman-level reading passages on topics like the relationship between hunting and art in the Paleolithic era and the role of women in the development of Japanese literature. Following each passage are multiple-choice questions that test your understanding of the information presented and the inferences that you draw from the material. The passages cover a variety of areas including: social studies, the natural sciences, prose fiction, and the humanities.

The Science Reasoning Test. You will read a series of reports on scientific experiments and mini-studies and then answer multiple-choice questions. There are three areas covered: data representation (graphs, tables, and diagrams); research summaries (descriptions of related experiments); and conflicting viewpoints (descriptions of related and contrary perspectives).

For a more detailed description of what each of these subject areas covers, refer to *Preparing for the ACT Assessment* available from your counselor or by writing to the address in Appendix A.

Duel Of The Three-Letter Acronyms: The SAT Vs. ACT

Unfortunately, we have a lapse in our powers of divination and can not predict on which test you will score higher. We can say that you can make an educated guess as to which test better suits you by understanding what they cover and how they are structured and scored. The main differences between the two exams are as follows:

Content

The SAT has a stronger emphasis on vocabulary.

The ACT tests grammar and punctuation. The SAT does not.

The ACT contains the Science Reasoning Test which covers the use of data representation, research summaries, and conflicting viewpoints in the natural sciences. The SAT does not.

About 7% of the ACT math questions are based on trigonometry. The SAT does not test trigonometry.

Structure

The test questions on the SAT get increasingly harder within each section. They do not on the ACT.

The ACT is all multiple choice. The SAT has "Student-Produced Response" mathematics questions.

The SAT has one experimental section that does not count toward your score. The ACT does not.

Both tests are about three hours long. The ACT has 215 questions while the SAT has about 140, meaning that you will have less average time to spend on each question on the ACT.

Scoring

There is a slight penalty for wrong answers on the SAT. There is none on the ACT.

For the ACT there are scores for the four components of the test and a composite score that is the average of the four scores. The SAT is broken into the Math score and the Verbal score.

Our advice: Take the practice exams in the test booklets and opt for whichever makes you feel most confident.

Advanced Placement Tests (APs)

Advanced Placement exams (APs) are the only exams that have the potential to make your parents love you more than they already do. You see, if you take enough of these tests, which allow you to earn college credit, you can knock a year off your college career. Which of course also means knocking a year's worth of tuition off your parents' tab.

APs are different from the other exams: They can be taken any time during high school and they are not required by colleges. Many schools offer courses to prepare for the exams, although you don't have to take an AP course in order to take a test. The benefits of taking these exams are of course being able to earn college credit without even stepping onto a college campus as well as being able to impress admissions officers with your ability to handle college level coursework. If you have taken some honors or AP courses you should take a few AP exams in the areas where you are strong even if you don't intend to graduate early. Again, they demonstrate to the colleges that you can handle college coursework.

The AP exams are scored on a scale of 1 to 5, with 5 signifying that you are practically ready to *teach* your own course on the subject and 1 basically signifying that you wrote your name on the exam. (Most colleges consider a score of 3 or higher a "passing" grade.) AP tests are given in the following areas:

Art: History of Art
Art: Studio Art
Biology
Calculus AB & BC
Chemistry
Computer Science

Economics: Macroeconomics
Economics: Microeconomics
English: English Language & Composition
English: English Literature & Composition
English: International English Language
Environmental Science
European History
French: French Language
French: French Literature
German Language
Government & Politics: United States
Government & Politics: Comparative
Latin
Music Theory
Physics
Psychology
Spanish: Spanish Language
Spanish: Spanish Literature
Statistics
U.S. History

TOEFL, TWE, And TSE

The Test of English as a Foreign Language (TOEFL), Test of Written English (TWE), and Test of Spoken English (TSE) measure English proficiency. They are for foreign students whose native language is not English and some residents who are recent immigrants to this country.

TOEFL. Over 2,400 colleges and universities in the U.S. require TOEFL scores for incoming foreign students, and it is administered in 180 countries around the world. The three sections of the multiple-choice test are: Listening Comprehension, Structure and Written Expression, and Reading Comprehension.

TWE. Administered with the TOEFL on selected test dates, the TWE requires you to write an essay in two pages or less on a provided topic.

TSE. The TSE is administered separately from the TOEFL and TWE. Designed to test your oral proficiency, it requires no writing. You will read and listen to questions on tape and then record your responses.

For more information on the TOEFL, TWE, and TSE and registration materials, ask your counselor or write to TOEFL/TSE Services. The address is in Appendix A.

How To Increase Your Scores By 100 Points Or More

If you are like a friend of ours from Harvard who scored 1590 on the SAT and knows precisely which single question he missed, you have absolutely nothing to worry about. Maybe the next time around you'll achieve perfection.

If you are like the rest of the student population and have the need and desire to increase your score, there is plenty that you can do. In fact, following are the strategies that we used to increase our own SAT scores by over 100 points.

Before we get to the good stuff on how you can pump up your scores, you should know that preparation requires time: The earlier you begin preparing for the tests and becoming familiar with their formats, the higher your scores will be. If it's already too late to give yourself an early start (meaning that the time until the test can be measured in days or even hours), don't try to cram but just focus on staying calm, becoming as familiar as possible with the structure and directions of the exams, and doing the best you can. If you do have several weeks or months before the tests the following is what you should do.

How To Best Prepare For Standardized Tests

Get friendly with your test booklets. The booklets provided by the test makers will be your best resource. You will not only be able to take a previous exam, but you will also learn test-taking tips from the test gurus themselves.

Become familiar with the format, content, and timing of the exams. Figure out how long it takes you to complete a section. Try to get a feel for when you have spent too long on one question and should move on. Don't forget to study the answer sheet, especially the answer grid for the SAT Math section!

Know the directions by heart. By knowing the directions you won't have to waste valuable time reading them during the exam.

Take exams (actual ones previously given if possible) for practice. You can probably think of about a gazillion other things you'd rather do in your free time than take tests, but unfortunately, there is no better way to prepare for these tests than to take them for practice. And there are no better tests to take than those that have actually been given.

Look for the books from The College Board with the acorn emblem on the cover. One of these books, *8 Real SATs*, has, as you may have guessed, 8 past SAT I exams. There is also an SAT II book that has one of each of the subject exams offered. It is best to take these real previous tests because they will be most similar to the actual exams that you will take.

For the other exams, scout out your local bookstore for test preparation books. With the hundreds of titles available, you will have no problem finding one for your test.

Don't cheat! Take the practice tests under the same conditions as the actual test. Time each section and stop when you are supposed to. Don't use dictionaries, books, or other aids to check your answers. Don't take a break in the middle of a section to watch a TV show and then come back to it later. Even use a number two pencil and fill in the ovals on the answer sheet, and practice with the calculator that you will use on the real test.

Grade your tests. Look at the questions you missed and see why you missed them. You may see a pattern develop after taking several practice tests and may want to review the material you don't know as well. If you ran out of time before you finished, try to figure out which areas took the most time. It may be better to save these parts until last and do the areas that you know you can answer more quickly first. Remember that the SAT I questions are arranged in an ascending order of difficulty. Yet, they are all worth the same points. So do the easy ones first and when you have extra time tackle the harder ones.

Review old notes and textbooks. It would be great if we could remember everything that we once read, knew, or learned, but unfortunately, as we all know from the experience of cramming the night before for exams, we can't. Thus it is necessary, especially for the Math, AP, and SAT II exams, to dig out your forgotten notes and dustball-covered textbooks from years before to review.

Identify and work on foreign material. You may have taken a course on one of the AP or SAT II Subject Tests, but you may not have covered all of the material that is included on the test (or you may not remember it even if you did). Cover it now.

Think about coughing up a few hundred bucks for a review class. Want to raise your SAT I score by 150 points? How much are you willing to pay? As you probably already know there are a countless number of businesses that are designed to prepare students for standardized tests. They often specialize in courses for the SAT I, and some of them even promise that your scores, as determined by tests they have designed, will increase by a specific number of points.

It would be really nice if the businesses could always deliver on their promises and if you had the several hundred dollars or so to pay for the course. Unfortunately, not every business delivers, and not everyone has this kind of spare change.

Still, don't rule out test preparation courses. If you do have the money or you can convince your parents that this is a worthy investment, test preparation courses are good for students who find it difficult to motivate themselves to study on their own. Some of them also offer some helpful shortcuts beyond just reviewing the material.

We suggest that you take advantage of the free introductions that many of the test preparation businesses offer even if you don't plan to take the course. During these introductory meetings, they usually offer tips and hints that you can't find in your textbooks. You'll also have the opportunity to take a practice exam under real test-taking conditions. By attending an introductory meeting, you will get a better idea of whether a test preparation course is for you. Best of all, it's free!

Don't overlook test preparation courses offered by your school or local college. Many high schools offer some form of free after-school test prep. If your school does not, make such a suggestion to your teachers and administration.

Set up your own review schedule. Of course, you can always prep yourself. But you will need to be serious and disciplined to do so. If you decide to do this then set up a study schedule with specific dates when you will give yourself real tests under actual conditions. And, needless to say, make sure you religiously stick to your plan.

How To Master Verbal And Reading Tests

Read like crazy. The more you read, the faster you'll read, which is important for the SAT I Critical Reading questions and ACT Reading Test. Start reading everything you can, covering as many subject areas, writing styles, and viewpoints as possible. Always read with a dictionary and look up unfamiliar words. Be sure to read works that are of literary merit and that cover a broad range of subjects such as *The New Yorker, New York Times, National Geographic, Newsweek,* or *Harper's.*

Study vocabulary as often as you brush your teeth. (Which we hope is at least three times a day!) The secret to success for the Verbal and Reading Tests is vocabulary, pure and simple. Even though they may not test vocabulary directly, it is essential to scoring well on the reading comprehension, sentence structure analysis, and writing tests.

Since brushing your teeth is theoretically part of your daily routine, add to this routine the study of vocabulary. It may sound difficult to do, but it's really not as bad as you may think. For example, you can carry around a deck of flash cards on which you write words and their meanings that you didn't know. Then while you are waiting for the bus or during the commercials of your favorite TV show you can whip them out and knock off a few. (More on this a little later.)

Use a vocabulary builder book. There are literally thousands of books offering different methods for remembering vocabulary words. Select the method that works best for you and use it. Set a goal—1 chapter or 25 words a week or whatever is realistic for you —and, most important, stick to it.

Study etymology, the origins of words. By studying etymology, you can learn the historical roots of words. Often these roots can be used to figure out the meaning of the words that you don't know. In fact, by understanding how these root words combine you can often figure out the meaning of hundreds of other words.

If all this root talk is confusing you, take a look at the following example. By studying etymology, you would learn that "bio" means life and "log" means the study of. Hence, "biology" is the study of life. Now you may have already known this, but with etymology you could also figure out (or at least take a good guess at) the meanings of such words as "biosphere," "biorhythm," "toxicology," "microbiology," "symbiosis," "sociology," "astrology," and "ethnology." By studying a few roots you can decipher a tremendous number of other words. A great etymology-based book to try is *Word Power Made Easy*.

Carry flashcards wherever you go. As mentioned earlier, make vocabulary flashcards of unknown words, and carry them *everywhere*. That way you can make the most of your time studying while standing in line, waiting for the bus, or even during a boring class (although don't let your teacher know). You'd be surprised how many words you can learn in your spare time.

Get mom and dad involved. To help motivate you to follow through on your plans to study new vocabulary offer mom and dad the following proposition. Using one or more of the above methods, if you manage to meet your goal of learning X number of words per week they reward you with $5 for that week. By the time your exam rolls around you will not only be ready to ace the verbal section but will have accumulated a sizable nest egg!

If your parents won't go for this deal then consider paying yourself $5 a week to be used for anything you want after you take the test.

Remember that words can have multiple meanings. You may be thinking of one definition of a word while the test makers may have another in mind. Make sure you study the various definitions of a word since often on the harder questions the test makers will use the less common meaning of a word.

Practice timed essay-writing. While writing practice essays in your spare time may not be your definition of fun, we guarantee it will help you improve your scores. Timed essays are not only a major part of the SAT II Writing Test and several other SAT II and AP tests but also of college mid-terms and finals. To prepare for the standardized test essays, gather the essay questions from previous tests, and practice writing essays within the given time limit. Here are some tips for timed essay-writing for tests:

Have something to say. You can be an incredibly talented writer, but without an idea to express, your essays will flop. And you'd be surprised to learn just how many decent writers bomb the test because they simply don't have an idea to convey. Make sure your essay has a point and clearly defined thesis statement.

Think of several canned introductions that can be applied to a variety of topics. Find a few quotes (but ones that are not so well known that they have become clichés) that you could use to start your essay. Also think of a few good analogies.

I (Jim Good) liked the analogy of the "keystone," which if you know something about architecture, was the final stone placed in old stone bridges and archways to hold the whole structure together. It was fairly easy to compare something to the "keystone," explaining how such-and-such a topic exemplified "keystone" qualities. Thinking of a few canned introductions will save you time and let you concentrate on the body of the essay, which is really where you should devote most of your writing time.

Keep your essays clear and organized. Because the test graders are required to read a number of essays, they are not able to give each piece as much time as they deserve. Help your ideas jump out at the readers by underlining your main points, especially if you have written a rather complex essay. If you run out of time when writing your essays, write a quick outline of your remaining points. This way the grader will know where you were headed and will most likely give you some points for it. But better yet, practice and prepare so you don't run out of time.

Find a kind soul to read your work. It might be helpful if you get some feedback on your essay writing style from someone else. An English teacher would be a perfect source of advice on how to improve your timed essays. Show some of your samples and ask for any suggestions for improvement.

For Reading Comprehension, sneak a peek at the questions first. If you read the questions quickly before the passage you will have a basic idea of what you will be looking for when you read. Note: Some students find that reading the questions first does not help them since it takes too much time. So, it would be best to try practicing both ways before you actually take the test.

Mark key parts when reading so you can find them easily when you are answering the questions. Certain words like "but," "however," and "except for" can change completely the meaning of a sentence. When you encounter these words, mark them in your test booklet. If an answer looks like it comes from one of these sentences, be extra sure you know what the sentence actually means.

Note the style and attitude of the writer in reading passages. Knowing this could help you select the correct answers by better understanding the author's point of view on a subject. Plus, there is almost always a question that asks you to guess the author's opinion or to select an appropriate title for the passage, both of which require that you have understood the author's position and attitude. This tip will help not only with Verbal, Reading, and English tests but also with the ACT Science Reasoning Test.

For SAT I Analogy questions, identify a precise relationship between the pair of capitalized words. Use both the words in a sentence or phrase. For example: if the words are APPLE: FRUIT you might make a sentence like: "An apple is a type of fruit." Now that you have identified the relationship, you can plug into this sentence the words from the answer choices. Ask yourself, "Is X a type of Y?" If you find that several answers meet this criteria then devise a more precise sentence to refine the relationship.

For the Sentence Completion questions, look at one blank at a time. If one word of a two-word pair does not fit into the sentence, that answer choice is incorrect and you can cross it out immediately. Quickly eliminate the answers that don't fit and then deal with your remaining choices.

Read your answer (silently) to yourself. After you have selected your answer double check that it is correct, especially for the Analogy and Sentence Completion questions.

Do the quicker questions first on the SAT I Verbal. Since all questions are worth the same amount of points, you will probably want to do the ones that take you less time (usually Analogies and Sentence Completions) before the ones that take longer.

Number Hunching And Number Crunching: How To Be A Math Whiz

You may be more creative than the test makers. When taking practice exams, you may discover that you found the answer in a different way from the answer key. That's okay. There are often several ways to arrive at the correct answer. What's important is not *how* you get it but *what* you get.

Memorize your algebra and geometry formulas. Make a song of them, hypnotize yourself, or chant them for 15 minutes a day. We don't care how you do it, just make sure you know your formulas cold. Although all the formulas you'll need will be given in the test booklet, don't rely on them since it will only waste your time flipping back and forth between pages. Plus, memorizing the formulas will help you to understand how to actually use them.

Experiment with different methods for solving problems. For some math problems that involve complicated formulas or a number of steps, it is easier to work backwards. To do this, plug the possible answers into the problem. When you are taking practice tests, figure out if this method works for you, and if it does, on which kinds of problems.

Plug in numbers for variables. On problems with complicated formulas with a number of variables, it can be faster to plug in actual numbers for each variable than to use formulas to figure out what the variables are.

Estimate if you can. If you see that the answers vary widely, use rounded off numbers in your calculations. For example, you can round off 4,867 X 6,732 to 5,000 X 7,000, which would give you 35,000,000. By estimating, you can easily eliminate choices that are not close to 35 million such as 35,000 or 35 billion.

Beware of the traps. When they write the test, test makers include a number of traps that catch most students. Your job is to not be fooled. Typical tricks test makers try to get away with include: giving more information than you need to solve a problem, offering incorrect choices that you can arrive at by partially completing the problem or by using the correct information with wrong calculations, and giving numbers in the answer choices that remind you of numbers in the equation. Be cautious of answers that are too easy to calculate, especially at the end of the SAT Math section when the problems are supposed to be the most difficult.

Know how to answer the SAT I Student-Produced Response questions. There are no negative answers or answers greater than 9,999. Percentages must be filled in as .75 or 3/4, NOT 75.

The Day Before The Big Event

Review the directions and answer sheets.

Make sure your batteries are working for your calculator or any other devices you'll need (e.g., cassette player for SAT II: Language Subject Tests with Listening). Gather all of the materials you'll need: admission ticket, identification, number two pencils, erasers, calculator (two if possible), non-beeping wristwatch, snack, and cassette player with earphones (if needed for SAT II: Language Subject Test with Listening).

And don't forget to get lots of zzz's.

Test Time Tips

Knowing that your performance on the standardized tests will be used by admissions officers in their evaluation, it's perfectly natural for you to feel nervous when the actual day arrives. Try to calm your nerves by keeping in mind that your scores are only one factor of many that the admissions committee will take into account. If you are a junior or are taking the test early in your senior year, you will also be able to take the test again, if need be. When taking the exams, it is most important that you try to stay calm so that you can think clearly. The following are some things to think about during the actual exams.

Pace yourself. It is natural for you to be nervous when the test first starts, but try to remain focused. Neither sprint through the test nor lag behind. Keeping with the race analogy, pace yourself. If you speed through the exam, you will make careless errors. But if you take too much time on each question, you won't be able to finish. Since you will (hopefully) have taken a number of tests for practice already, you should know just how fast you need to go.

Tick tock. Watch the clock. Make a note of the finish time of each section so you can pace yourself and leave enough time to get to all the questions.

Read all questions carefully and completely. Don't start figuring out the answer until you have all the information.

Consider all of the choices. After you have found what you believe to be the correct answer, make sure that you look at the other choices, too. There may be a better answer. Realize that an answer by itself may be true, but it still may not be the answer to the question. You must select the BEST answer.

Cross out the choices you know are incorrect so that you don't waste time reading them again.

It's not your imagination; the questions do get increasingly harder on the SAT I and SAT II exams. Except for the SAT I Critical Reading section, the questions are arranged in increasing order of difficulty in each section. (In the Critical Reading section, the passages increase in difficulty, but the questions following the passages are in no particular order of difficulty.)

Knowing this, it is best for you to start at the beginning and answer the easier questions first. Remember that question #10 will be much harder than question #3. As you progress toward the end of the section, be very wary of answers that seem too easy since these will most likely be tricks and will not be correct.

If you can't get the answer, move on. Don't spend too much time on any one question. Mark ones you can't figure out, and come back to them if you have time at the end.

Don't be afraid to guess. For the ACT, guess even if you don't know the answer. There's no penalty! The same goes for the Student-Produced Response Questions.

For the rest of the SAT I and SAT II, guess if you know that one or more of the choices is incorrect. Don't ask us to explain the math behind this, but it's better to guess if you can eliminate at least one wrong answer. However, if you really don't have a clue what the answer is and cannot eliminate any of the choices, leave the question blank. Even by omitting a few questions, you can still receive a high score.

Mark up your test booklet. Underline key parts of reading passages. Circle key numbers in mathematical problems. Use the white space in your booklets to do calculations. The test graders are not judging you on how much you can do in your head, so mark up your test booklet as much as you want. Remember, only your answer sheet will be graded.

Don't mark up your answer sheet (where you're not supposed to). Extra lines or marks could confuse the grading machines and cost you points.

Bubble correctly. It's common sense but it's been done incorrectly often enough to merit mention. Make sure that you fill the correct bubble, especially when you skip questions.

Check your work if you have extra time.

Bring a snack. There will be a short break when you will be able to use the bathroom, get a drink of water, and commiserate with your fellow test-takers. At this time you may want to wolf down a satisfying *Snickers* to give you that burst of sugar-induced energy to get you through the second half of the exam.

A Timeline For Testing

The general rule for when you should take the ACT or SAT I is once during the spring of your junior year, and if you are not satisfied with your scores, again in the fall of your senior year.

For the SAT II, ideally you should take the subject tests soon after you have completed courses covering the subject because it is easy to forget how to conjugate "estar" in Spanish or the intimacies of the causes of the American Revolution.

The exception is when you are planning to take another course in the same subject area. If you are, you may want to take the test once, take the next course, and take the test again. For example, if you have taken three years of Latin and have a solid grasp of the language, you should probably take the SAT II Latin exam in your junior year. If you take a fourth year of Latin, you may want to take the exam again in your senior year as well.

If you plan to take exams again in the fall of your senior year, you should spend the summer before studying. Try to take the exams as early in the fall as you can because later in the fall you will be busy completing your actual applications and will not want to have to worry about taking more tests.

Here is a quick summary of when to take the tests:

PSAT: Definitely your junior year and maybe even earlier.

SAT I: Spring of junior year and fall of senior year.

ACT: Spring of junior year and fall of senior year

SAT II: As soon as possible after you have taken the related courses, unless you will take a more advanced related course.

APs: As soon as possible after you have taken the related courses.

Remember that if you plan to apply Early Action, you will need to take your exams as early as possible. Check with each school for their deadline to make sure that you take the exams in time.

Three's A Crowd: Only Take Exams Twice

Studies have shown that students' scores typically increase some amount the second time. If, however, you do very well and score in the 600s or 700s on your exams, celebrate! You probably shouldn't take them again unless you honestly think you can improve. Your high scores might seem less valid if you score lower the second time around.

Whether you choose to take the exams again or not, do not take them more than twice. Chances are your scores will not improve after a second time, and it does not impress admissions officers to see that you have three test dates each resulting in similarly low scores. Plus, you'd probably much rather enjoy sleeping in on a Saturday morning than taking a test for the third time.

How To Deal With A Bombed Test

It's not the end of the world if you don't do as well on a test as you expected. If you have the time, you can take the test again. If not, then try not to worry (what's done is done) and instead spend the rest of your time writing a killer application. Concentrate on getting good grades and finding teachers who will write strong evaluations. You can prove to a college that you are academically capable in ways other than test scores. Remember that lots of students admitted into America's top schools have less-than-perfect test scores.

HOW TO WIN FREE CASH FOR COLLEGE

11

In This Chapter
- ▲ Why Money Is Everything & How To Get Some
- ▲ Financial Aid Mumbo Jumbo Explained
- ▲ Stories From Real Life: How I Paid For College $150 At A Time
- ▲ Great Sources Of Free Cash For School
- ▲ Map To The Financial Aid Jackpots
- ▲ How To Write A Winning Scholarship Essay
- ▲ Negotiating More Money From Colleges

Money Is Everything

One student we know was presented with a tempting proposal after he was accepted to Harvard. His parents told him that they would either:

A) Pay for him to go to Harvard or

B) Pay for him to go to a much cheaper state university AND buy him a brand new Mercedes.

Of course this student chose to go to Harvard and by his senior year had finally saved up enough money to buy a very used Hyundai Excel. The point of this story is to emphasize (in terms we can all relate to) the truly incredible cost of college. This student's parents would have spent *much less* had he chosen Option B. In fact they would have had to purchase FOUR Mercedes before they would even come close to spending what it would cost for a Harvard education.

The stark reality is that the annual cost of college (and private schools are especially guilty) is *more than what some families earn in an entire year.* And, as if that were not bad enough, the cost is continuing to rise. So, of course, it makes sense that when speaking about a college education, money is a major concern. For some, money is the most important factor of all.

Luckily, colleges and the government can help you foot the bill. In fact, last year financial aid for students totaled over $50 billion. However, despite this promising number, do not expect your college to simply hand over a stack of bills. It's going to take a little work to get a piece of this financial aid pie.

In this chapter, we will show you how to squeeze the most money out of the schools, government, and private scholarships. And who knows, if you are able to save your parents a ton of money on college tuition and prevent them from taking out a second mortgage, they just might buy you that new car for graduation!

Financial Aid Mumbo Jumbo Explained

Applying for financial aid is very much like filling out tax forms. While there is a lot of technical mumbo jumbo, there are a few essential concepts and terms which you need to know in order to understand the process.

The first thing to understand is that financial aid comes in various forms from the government, colleges, and private organizations. These include:

Grants Or Scholarships–Money with no strings attached–meaning you don't have to pay it back. This is really the equivalent of hitting the financial aid jackpot.

Federal Work-Study (FWS)–(Formerly College Work-Study) The government will help subsidize your salary for jobs during the semester. This means you will have an easy time finding work on and off campus since you will be cheap labor (your employer will only have to pay part of your salary, with the government picking up the rest.) The downside is, of course, that since you will have to work you will have less time to goof off!

How I Paid For College $150 At A Time

I used to think that if I could be born again I'd want to be a Trump, Gates, or Rockefeller. It's not that I have such expensive tastes that I need more money than I could possibly spend (although that would be nice), but when I realized how much it would cost to go to college it seemed like you practically had to be an heir or heiress to afford it.

I come from a middle class family. My parents are both elementary school teachers, and I have never had to seriously worry about money before. As a child I may not have gotten Barbie's Dream Mansion for Christmas, but I did always get a new Barbie doll.

So when it came time to apply for college I was shocked when my parents had their first serious talk about money with me. They told me that after checking their finances, they couldn't afford to send me to an expensive private school unless I could find a way to raise about $8,000 a year on my own. A summer job and working part time during the school year would take care of about half that amount, but I was still short by $4,000.

Since I really wanted to go to a private college, I knew I had to find a way to get the money. I visited my counselor, who advised me to apply for some scholarships. I was surprised to find that there were quite a few scholarships available, ranging from the local Lions Club to the Kodak Film Company. I applied for every scholarship that I thought fit me. I had my doubts, however, and each time I mailed off a completed application I wondered if I was wasting my time.

Was I shocked when I actually won awards from 9 groups for varying amounts between $150 and $2,000. In total I won over $5,000! What really made the difference were the little awards for $150 to $500 which added up quickly. With this money I was able attend an elite (and expensive) private school.

Now that I am in college I continue to apply for scholarships. Sure it takes time to complete the applications, but each little award counts and helps to ease the burden on my parents. I've learned that if you make the effort, you can make almost any school affordable. The money is there—you just need to put in the work to get it.

By: Jenny M. who happily accepts any amount of free money.

Low-Interest Or Deferred-Interest Loans–These are the easiest to qualify for but that's because they must be paid back with interest. However, you will find that the terms can be fairly generous. To receive these you complete a loan application. When your application is approved, you sign a promissory note, promising to repay the money.

Individual states also award money, usually through their education agencies. State aid includes the State Student Incentive Grant (SSIG) Program and the Robert C. Byrd Honors Scholarship Program. To find out which state education agency to contact, ask the colleges' financial aid office or the U.S. Department of Education.

There are also two general criteria for getting money for college. The first is called *need based.* From the various financial aid forms that you submit, the colleges and government will determine how much you (that's right you are expected to contribute to your own education) and your parents can afford to pay. The difference between this number and the annual cost of your college education will be your financial need, which will be met by a combination of grants, work-study, and loans.

The second criterion is *merit based.* Merit based aid is awarded for skills or talents that are not related to students' financial need. For example, students can win scholarships from colleges based on their athletic, leadership, or academic achievement.

Besides money from colleges and the government, another important source of financial aid is *outside scholarships.* These can be need based, merit based or both and are sponsored by various private groups. Outside scholarships often require the most work but are also some of the more lucrative. Proof: One student we know won over $100,000 in merit-based outside scholarships!

Money From Uncle Sam

If you've ever wondered where your parents' hard-earned taxes paid to the government goes, here's part of the answer. A significant chunk of it goes toward funding student financial aid programs. This is your golden opportunity to get back some of your parents' tax dollars.

Almost all government aid is based on financial need, except for unsubsidized Stafford loans, PLUS loans, and Consolidation loans. Here are some descriptions of the various types of federal aid for which you may qualify:

Federal Pell Grants–These are grants for undergraduate students who have not earned a bachelor's or professional degree. Every student who is eligible receives this grant. The average award is around $2,350 per student.

Federal Stafford Loans–Stafford Loans are available through two programs: the William D. Ford Federal Direct Loan (Direct Loan) Program, in which you receive funds directly from the U.S. Government; and through the Federal Family Education Loan (FFEL) Program, in which you receive funds from a bank, credit union, or other lender that participates in the program. These loans also come in two forms: *subsidized*, awarded based on financial need in which the government pays the interest for the loan until you begin to pay it off, and *unsubsidized*, in which you owe the interest as soon as you take out the loan. Typically, you begin to repay Stafford Loans as soon as you graduate or leave school.

Federal PLUS Loans–These are loans for your parents which are available through both the Direct Loan and FFEL programs. Your parents will begin repaying the loan about two months after the final loan disbursement your senior year, which means that they will begin repaying the loan while you are still in school.

Federal Consolidation Loans–These are loans that combine the different federal student loans that you receive so that it is simpler for you to repay them.

The following types of aid are Campus-Based Programs, which means that they are administered by the college financial aid offices. The colleges are responsible for disbursing the funds they receive from the government for each program.

Federal Supplemental Educational Opportunity Grants (FSEOG)–These grants are awarded to students with the greatest financial need. Unlike Pell Grants, there is no guarantee that every eligible student will receive this type of grant because of their limited availability.

Federal Work-Study (FWS)–This program will help provide you with a job so that you can work and study at the same time. Most jobs are on campus, although some, which usually involve work with nonprofit or public agencies, are not.

Federal Perkins Loans–These are low-interest loans for students with great financial need. Although the money for these loans comes from the government, you pay back the loan to the college after you graduate or leave school.

For more detailed information on federal aid programs, get a copy of *The Student Guide To Financial Aid* from the U.S. Department of Education from your counselor, or check Appendix A for the address of where to write for a copy.

All The Forms You Need To Fill

You will not appreciate the true monotony of filling out forms until you have finished applying for financial aid. You will calculate so many figures and fill in so many blanks that you will be begging for multiple-choice answers like those on the SAT.

Fortunately, while applying for financial aid from the colleges and the government is a tedious process, it is not terribly difficult. From the multitude of forms you need to complete and submit, colleges and the government want to determine your financial need. For federal aid, this figure is arrived at by subtracting the Cost of Attendance (COA), the estimated annual cost of the college including tuition, room and board, books and supplies, and travel expenses from your Expected Family Contribution (EFC), the amount you and your parents can reasonably contribute:

Cost of Attendance (COA)
− Expected Family Contribution (EFC)

= Financial Need

You will need your parents' help in filling out the forms since they ask for tax return information and details of your family's assets and liabilities. The following is a list of the major forms that you will need to complete:

Financial Aid Form–Most colleges have their own form for you to complete with information about you and your family. The colleges basically want to know your available assets–such as that $20 million trust fund. However, this form also has a section where you can explain (often by attaching a separate letter) any special circumstances–such as an impending layoff of one of your parents–that would affect your family's finances. Be sure to talk to your parents about this and don't be afraid to honestly describe your family's financial situation.

Free Application For Federal Student Aid (FAFSA)–The government will use information from this form about you and your family to calculate your financial need and report the results to the colleges you have selected. After you are admitted you will receive an aid package that may consist of grants, loans, and work-study based on your need.

This form is for U.S. citizens, permanent residents, and eligible non-citizens. It is generally available in December from your high school counseling office and often from the college financial aid offices, as well. It should be completed as soon *after* January 1 as possible. The deadline for submitting the FAFSA for colleges to use it in their consideration is usually February 1, but it can be earlier if you are applying for state aid. Approximately one month after you submit the FAFSA, you will receive a Student Aid Report (SAR), which will indicate your Expected Family Contribution. See Appendix A for where to write for a FAFSA form or for *FAFSA Express,* software you can use to complete the form electronically.

College Scholarship Service (CSS) Financial Aid PROFILE Service–About 900 colleges, universities, and scholarship programs accept or require this service for awarding aid. To register for PROFILE, get a registration form from your high school counselor, college financial aid office, or use the College Board's *ExPan* software, which may be available at your school. In general, you should register as soon as possible. After you receive the PROFILE application, submit it as early as you can. Each college sets its own deadline, but the earliest deadline for registering is usually December 15, and the last deadline for submitting the application is usually February 1. For early action, the deadlines are about two to three months earlier.

Federal Income Tax Returns–The IRS isn't the only one who wants these. The colleges need copies of your parents' and your federal tax forms and W-2 forms. Usually you can submit estimates and turn in the actual forms later.

Business/Farm Supplement–A part of the PROFILE application, this form is required of all students whose parents own a business or farm. Some colleges may require their own form instead of or in addition to the PROFILE form.

Divorced/Separated Parent Statement–Required from the non-custodial parent, this form is also in the PROFILE application. Some colleges may also require you to complete one of their own forms.

Now that you know everything you need to fill out, sign, and submit, you might not want to do it. Resist this temptation. Even if you do not think you qualify for financial aid, it doesn't hurt to apply. You may find that the work-study and low-interest loans are just what you need to round out your ability to pay your tuition.

A Note For International Applicants

If you are not a U.S. citizen, you may have somewhat less opportunities for aid. To receive aid from the U.S. government, you must be a citizen, U.S. national, or permanent resident. Very specific groups of non-citizens are also eligible. Still, your own government may have funds to help, and many American colleges provide aid to international students as well.

For more information on aid for international students, get a copy of *Funding for U.S. Study: A Guide for Foreign Nationals.* See Appendix A for the address.

Most colleges will request that you complete the following: CSS Foreign Student Financial Aid Application (FSFAA) and Certificate of Finances (COF). These are available from the college financial aid or admissions offices. Some colleges require their own financial aid forms for international students instead of or in addition to these forms. You should refer to the individual applications for more information. Exceptions to this are students who are not

U.S. citizens or permanent residents but whose parents live or earn income in the U.S. If you are in this category, most colleges will ask you to use the PROFILE service instead.

Tips For Filling Out The Forms

Here are some important guidelines to keep in mind while filling out the myriad of forms.

▶ **Be Thorough.** By this we mean both making sure that you complete every blank and that you include as much information as you have.

▶ **Be Honest.** You don't want lies about your financial aid application coming to haunt you as a student. And trust us, you won't be a student for long if this happens.

▶ **Show That You Need Aid (If Indeed You Do).** If you are in need of support, which is the case for most students, demonstrate it. In the space provided on the application or in a separate letter, explain any factors that you think might affect your family's ability to pay. Make sure to note any extenuating circumstances that the government or colleges may overlook. Such circumstances include unusual medical or dental expenses, costs for a sibling's education, or a parent's recent unemployment.

▶ **Make Copies As Cheat Sheets.** After you have completed all of your application forms, make sure that you make copies of them. You will be using some of this information when applying to other scholarships and also when applying for aid for the following year. You've been through the grueling process once, make it easier for yourself the next time by having your photocopies to use as cheat sheets.

Outside Scholarships: The Best Free Cash In The World

Money for future circus performers. Money for left-handed students. Money for children of Republicans. Outside scholarships award money for every kind of family background, interest, and skill imaginable. Unlike college and government aid, many outside scholarships are based solely on students' academic and personal achievements rather than financial need. Plus, some are renewable for all four years of college.

However, don't count on a free ride just yet. Most of these outside scholarships are competitive, but if you are willing to spend a few evenings completing the application forms, you will have a good chance of winning some of this free cash for school.

Map To The Financial Aid Jackpots

The best place to find these sources of free cash is in your own community. Usually your Lions, Rotary, Kiwanis, American Legion, and other civic groups offer scholarships to local high school students. To find out where and when you need to apply, check with your guidance counselor or call or write the groups directly. Your guidance counselor will be particularly knowledgeable about local and regional scholarships. Keep in touch with him or her so that you will know what's available.

Every library has several books listing literally thousands of scholarships. You should spend a day sorting through these tomes and picking out the scholarships that you have a good chance of winning. Pay special attention to the restrictions since many scholarships are limited to specific groups of students, such as third generation Irish Americans whose fathers worked in shipyards.

Also, there are now some great sites on the Internet that have searchable listings of scholarships. Check out Appendix B for the best ones.

Strategies For Winning Scholarships

Once you find some scholarships to apply for, follow these strategies to maximize your chances.

Apply To Those That Fit You Best. Don't let visions of dollar signs dancing in your head color your judgment. Groups that provide scholarships print guidelines and restrictions for a reason: They follow them. If you find a scholarship for students who plan

How I Got My School To Give Me More Money

I was ecstatic when I first opened the letter. I had been admitted to the Ivy League school of my dreams. However, my enthusiasm waned when my parents said that it was going to be difficult to pay for my education with only the small loan that the school offered. They wanted me to go to our state's public university instead, which had offered me a full scholarship. That was when I decided that I had to do every thing I could to sweeten the deal from the private school.

I wrote them a letter explaining my situation. I said that I would love to attend the Ivy League college but that the state university's offer of a full scholarship was difficult to refuse. Then, I asked if there was anything that they could do to make their offer more comparable. To my surprise the school responded by offering a $5,000 grant and a significantly larger loan. Of course I never told the financial aid officer that I would have attended the school even if they hadn't offered me anything else. But it sure would have been difficult on my family had I not negotiated more aid.

By: Christina A. who is now a happy Ivy Leaguer and whose parents are even happier that they are not broke.

Stories From Real Life Stories From Real Life Stories From Real Life

to be future journalists, don't apply when the closest you have come to journalism was writing a letter to the editor of the school newspaper. There will be a lot of students out there who have written for their school newspapers since they were in kindergarten, and they will win the money. No matter how big the jackpot, don't apply for scholarships for which you do not meet the guidelines and restrictions.

Check Out The Competition. Before you decide to apply, know who your competition will be. It may be better for you to concentrate your energy on applying to regional scholarships rather than national scholarships. In regional scholarships you will be competing against the best students in your city or county, which will be tough; but competing nationally will be even tougher. Of course, don't rule out national scholarships. Many national scholarships offer significantly higher support than regional scholarships. After all, someone has to win these cash cows and it might as well be you.

Be Realistic About Your Financial Need. If you apply for a scholarship that is based on financial need, be truthful about how great your financial need really is. If it's clear on paper that you really don't need the funds, don't waste your time applying for a scholarship that will be awarded to someone who does.

How To Write A Winning Scholarship Essay

If you think that writing essays for college applications was an exhausting experience, we're sorry to break the bad news to you—there are more to come. Many scholarship applications require at least one essay—although they are usually (but not always) shorter than those for college admissions.

Before you begin wondering if it's worth the trouble to apply, the good news is that because you have already written quality essays for your college applications, you have some very good recycling possibilities. Plus this time you have the motivation of writing to be *paid* money instead of writing to *spend* money as you did for the college application essays.

Similar to admissions officers, scholarship committees see the essay as a window into the hearts and minds of the applicants. Because of this, essays for scholarships should be written similarly to college essays. They should be original, well-written, honest, and describe something meaningful about you. Scholarship essays should captivate the readers and make them care about the writer. All the strategies that you learned in the college essay writing chapters also apply to scholarship essays.

While a scholarship application may give you the luxury of writing on any subject—in which case you can easily submit one of your college essays—most give you a much more focused topic. For example, if you are applying to an organization dedicated to promoting world peace they may ask you to write about—what a coincidence—world peace. If you are applying to a civic group, they may ask you to write about your volunteer experience. In these cases you need to demonstrate in your essay that you are strong in that particular field or area or that you are the most suitable candidate because you fulfill the specific criteria of the award better than anyone else.

This may mean that you will have to write a new essay. However, since these essays are shorter and it is not expected (like the college application essays) that you spend weeks on them, they should be much easier to turn out. Once you get going you can usually whip out an essay pretty quickly, especially if you can cut and paste one together from several previous essays.

The final thing you should keep in mind when writing is to consider the kinds of people who will be reading your essay. An essay about how you wished you were born in a communist country because of your love for Marx may not go over well for an American Legion scholarship—many of whose members risked their lives fighting communists. An essay about the evils perpetrated by big business may not find much sympathy in a scholarship committee composed of Rotarians. Keep in mind, at all times, who your readers will be and make sure what you write will not offend them.

Strategies To Milk More Money

This final section is for after you receive notice of your financial aid offer which will come from the colleges a few weeks after you get accepted.

Colleges do their best to provide financial aid packages that make their schools affordable, but there are times when their offer is not enough for even the most resourceful families to pay the bills. This is especially true when unexpected changes occur such as a parent being laid off or a family member becoming ill. When this happens you need to be honest with the school and tell them that their offer is simply not enough.

First, compose a letter in which you outline the reasons why you need more aid. When writing your reasons, be as specific as possible. For example, lay out your parents' annual income after taxes and how it is broken down to pay for your families' living expenses. Demonstrate how if your parents contribute as much as the college asks them to, they will be unable to meet the family's financial obligations. Also, explain any extenuating circumstances that might not be reflected in the information you submitted with the financial aid form.

Second, if you have received more aid from one school than another, you can try to use this difference as leverage. In other words, you can write a letter to College A asking them to match or at least increase your aid so that it is closer to the offer from College B. You should explain that you would like to attend College A, but that because College B has offered more aid, you may be forced to attend it out of financial necessity. While colleges may not always be able to increase your award, it is certainly worth the time writing a letter to try.

How To Write A Letter To Milk More Money

If you find it hard to believe that a single letter can result in a larger financial aid package, here is proof. The following is an actual letter one student wrote to the Harvard financial aid office. Before writing the letter, the student had received only a small loan from Harvard despite the fact that her father had been laid off for over a year. The student composed this letter to explain her family's extenuating circumstances, describing their actual income and expenses. Her letter paid off–she was awarded a $6,500 scholarship for the semester!

Letter To Harvard

Dear Sir or Madam:

I am writing to request that my financial aid package for the fall semester be reconsidered. My family and I were disappointed with the amount we were offered because in addition to my father having been unemployed for over a year, my older sister will be a sophomore in college; and my mother, a part-time teacher, has received no income since June because of summer break.

We understand that nearly every family must undergo an amount of hardship to send its members to college. However, because my parents wish to continue financing my sister's and my education, they are worried about how they will pay for their own expenses. They have been using my mother's income to basically cover their mortgage payments, and their savings to pay for everything else. In February, my parents had $33,000 in savings. In the last six months, their savings has decreased by about $15,000. They now have about $18,000 to contribute to my sister's and my college expenses as well as to spend on their and my younger brother's food and basic necessities. They don't know how long their savings will last without a change in the amount of aid I will receive.

At the end of this month, my sister will begin her sophomore year at USC. The cost will be $26,998, and she has received $18,758 in financial aid. This makes my parent's contribution amount to $8,240, of which they will borrow $2,625. One of the things you might be able to address is why my sister's financial aid package was dramatically higher than mine.

Since July of last year my father has been unemployed. His severance pay ended in October, and his unemployment benefits have been depleted since February. Although he has applied for over a dozen positions, his prospects for finding a job in his specialty are slim.

My parents and I have discussed the possibility of having me take a year off so that I may work to help pay for tuition, but we'd much rather that I begin now and work after I have received my degree.

Please contact my parents or me with any further questions you may have. Thank you very much for your time and consideration. I hope that this information is helpful in your review of my application.

Sincerely,

GET STARTED BEFORE YOUR SENIOR YEAR

● ●

FOR FRESHMEN, SOPHOMORES, & JUNIORS

In This Chapter
▲ **Everything You Need To Know About College Admissions**
▲ **How To Prepare A Winning Transcript & Resume**
▲ **Plan Your High School Years Right**
▲ **The Art Of Getting Teachers & Advisors To Adore You**
▲ **The Cure For Appliphobia**

Catch The Early Bird Worms

My (Lisa Lee) mother used to say in her inspired attempts to wake me, "The early bird catches the worm." My reply would always be, "I don't want any worms," as I rolled over in my bed and burrowed deeper beneath the covers. In the case of college admissions, trust me, this time you most definitely want the worm. In fact, you want a whole bucket of worms.

If you are a junior, sophomore, or even freshman reading this, then boy what a nerd you are! No, seriously, kudos to you! You are giving yourself an advantage that most seniors only *wish* that they had. There are so many things to do for college admissions that the earlier you start the more successful you will be. In this chapter we will look specifically at some of the things you can do now to raise your chances of getting in later.

Before we begin, however, we should warn you that your goal in getting an early start is to accomplish as much as possible. You don't have to do everything—if you did you would not have any time left to enjoy your pre-senior youth.

Everything An Underclassman Needs To Know About College Admissions (But Is Afraid To Ask)

You have a lot of important things on your mind right now—whom to go with to the prom, when you're going to pass your driving test, what's for dinner—but even with all these important life decisions to ponder, it is important for you to devote some time to thinking about where you want to apply to college. Most seniors have no idea where they want to go to school and often make hasty decisions. In Chapter 2, there is a list of factors that you should keep in mind when considering various colleges. But, of course, first you need some options.

Start now by asking your parents, teachers, counselors, older siblings, and friends about colleges. Talk to alumni from your high school about their experiences. Ask them about their courses, activities, and social life. Go to the library and check out one of those guides in the reference section that describe various colleges and universities. If you are wired, you can surf the Net and visit the homepages of some of the colleges. If your family is taking a summer trip, why not visit a few college campuses at the same time?

Having some idea of where you might want to apply will come in handy when it comes time to make the real decision. While you are considering various colleges, try to keep the following general questions in mind:

▶ What is the strength of the school's academic program, and does it offer courses in the fields in which you might be interested? (A school that is strong in computer science may have a terrible comparative literature department.) If you are unsure about what you might want to major in, then make sure you look for schools that have good programs all around. Remember, too, that while science may be your favorite subject now, you might find that in college there are more interesting ways to spend your time than cooped up in a lab.

▶ How is the campus environment? Is there a large or small student body? Is the school in the middle of a city or way out in the country? Do you like the climate? You can learn a lot just by visiting the schools and walking the campus. Also, information on class size and teacher to student ratios can be found in most college guide books. Of course, to get the real story on what the school is like you should try to talk to some alumni.

▶ What kind of social environment, including the kinds of activities, does the college offer? If hiking and fishing are hobbies that you need to stay sane, then you don't want to go to a school in the middle of an urban wasteland. (Then again some people find wastelands charming.)

Visit College Campuses

If flipping through brochures and dry college guides at the library does not give you a full enough picture of the colleges–which it shouldn't–another way to learn about them is to take a field trip. The next time your family goes on a vacation, check if you will be passing by any of the colleges you might want to attend. If you are, why not stop by for a short visit? While you're there take a campus tour, sit in on a class if you can, or just take a walk around the campus absorbing its ambiance. You can learn a lot from observing: the size and environment of the campus, what surrounds the campus, and how happy the students appear. It's still early and right now you just want to get a feel for your options and have a sense of what's out there.

By getting an early start on thinking about where you want to apply you will have a tremendous advantage when the time to apply really comes.

The Application? What's That?

Speaking of when the time comes, when you become a senior you will send for and receive the applications to the colleges where you might apply. In general, these applications do not vary much between schools. In fact, you can even look at this year's applications as a preview. College applications almost always include:

The Actual Application Form. This is a fun collection of blanks, spaces, and short questions about your education, test scores, family, activities, awards, and work experience.

Essays. Usually the colleges ask you to write your autobiography in the generous space of 500 words or less. Sometimes colleges will give you a choice of topics to write on, such as a memorable experience, a personal hero, or an issue that is important to you. Usually, there will also be one to four shorter questions that might ask you to write about your favorite extracurricular activity, book, or why you have chosen to apply to the college.

Evaluations. Better start getting onto the good side of everyone you know. Colleges usually require three or more evaluations from your teachers, counselors, and (maybe) even your boss.

The Interviews. These one-on-one discussions with an alumnus or admissions officer are the only time you will interact directly with a human being during the admissions process. (Note: Not all schools require the interview.)

Test Scores And Transcript. Most colleges require that you take the Scholastic Assessment Test I: Reasoning Test (SAT I) or ACT Assessment and three SAT II Subject Tests. It is also highly recommended that you take some Advanced Placement (AP) tests. You will also need to send each college a transcript listing your courses and grades.

For some of these parts, let the procrastinator in you rejoice because you really can't do much until your senior year. However, for the worm-hungry part of you, there are several things you can do right now. Beginning with:

Challenge Your Brain

One of the most important factors in being admitted to a selective college is, as your parents have probably lectured to you more times than you would like to remember, your grades. To get into the top colleges, you need to have a very competitive grade point average. This does not mean that you need straight "A's"; a few "B's" on a mostly "A" report card are fine.

However, be careful since not all grades are considered equal. Getting a "B" in an honors or Advanced Placement course is much better than getting an "A" in a non-honors course. After all, it's not fair to compare an "A" in home economics to an "A" in AP physics, is it? In fact, colleges often recalculate your GPA based on how many courses are honors or Advanced Placement.

Some students make the mistake of trying to get a 4.0 GPA by taking the easiest classes offered like, "Woodshop: How to Cut Wood." This is a big mistake and often costs them admission into a top school. College admissions officers want to see that you are motivated and willing to challenge yourself academically. At the earliest time possible you should sign up for honors and Advanced Placement classes. Yes, this will mean that you will be voluntarily asking for more homework, will spend more time studying, and will take more difficult tests, but an acceptance letter to a competitive school will be your reward.

Practice For And Take The Alphabet Soup Of Tests

There is no avoiding it. You will, before graduation, spend at least a dozen excitement-filled hours filling in bubbles while taking a battery of standardized tests that have names that sound like they were created in a bowl of alphabet soup. These tests will most likely include the PSAT, APs, SAT I or ACT, and SAT II Subject Tests. To learn what each of these mysterious combinations of letters stands for and for a cheat sheet on how to prepare for them, please take a look at Chapter 10.

You will notice that the tests are concentrated toward the end of your junior and beginning of your senior year. But some, like the PSAT, APs and SAT II Subject Tests, may be taken earlier. For example, if you finish a world history class in your sophomore year, you'll want to take the subject exam in world history while the material is still fresh. Things like the terms of the Treaty of Versailles tend to slip the mind quickly.

Your most immediate worry is probably the PSAT, which you can take in your sophomore and junior year. It is a practice test designed to get you ready for the real SAT I so in a sense you don't have to stress too much. However, the score from your junior year PSAT will be used to determine if you qualify for a National Merit Scholarship, which aside from the honor comes with a cash prize to help defray tuition at the school of your choice. So, it is worth taking the PSAT seriously and putting in some time to study for it as if it were the real SAT I.

While Chapter 10 has a whole list of suggestions for preparing for these tests the important thing to remember is to start early. Even if you don't consider reviewing your math book from last year or drilling yourself with reading comprehension passages a blast, convince yourself that taking some practice exams is a hoot. The real secret of all those high-priced test preparation services is that they force their students to get familiar with the test and become comfortable with the type of questions asked. This alone can boost your scores tremendously. Buy yourself a book of past exams and make it a habit to review it regularly.

Keep Active

By keeping active, we don't mean for you to run a few laps around the track. Rather, one of the more important things for you to do before your senior year is to make yourself look good on paper by staying busy with activities. Activities include clubs and organizations, sports, student government, and volunteer work. While many of these activities will be connected with your school, feel free to get involved with community-based activities as well.

When applying to college, you will find that much of your application is not only based on your classroom life but also on your out-of-classroom life. You will be given a chance to brag about your extracurricular activities on the application form, and most students find that they use some experience connected with these activities in part of their college essay.

To really "woo" the admissions officers, you will need to become a leader in some of your activities or even start a club or group of your own. There is nothing more impressive to admissions officers than students who take initiative. In fact, more important than what particular activity you choose to participate in is the quality of your participation, meaning how much you contribute as a member and leader.

Run for office in clubs or the school government. Try to be the captain of your sports team. Volunteer to head a project for your service organization. Start a group or club of your own. This will demonstrate your leadership skills as well as your ability to take initiative. Also, try to stick with the activities you enjoy for a number of years. It's important to show that you are dedicated. Membership in the Yoga Club for four straight years, for example, is certainly a reflection of dedication. It is also the only way to become a leader.

Compete To Stand Out

It should be no surprise to you that colleges like winners. In fact, on the college application form, there is a section for listing all of your awards and honors. These include both academic awards like the county-wide spelling bee and nonacademic honors like grand prize in a ukulele playoff. Thus, it makes sense that for every competition or contest you have a chance at winning, you need to compete. Luckily, there is an abundance of competitions out there for you to win. These include speech, writing, art, musical, scientific, debate, athletic, and more. Watch for the competitions that you think you have a chance of winning, and take the time to enter them. Keep in mind that winning does not necessarily mean taking first place. Being a runner-up in a state or national competition is just as impressive as winning a local award.

There are even many awards that you do not have to officially enter to win. For example, your teacher may award you a certificate for being Super Math Citizen of the Month or your school may vote you Outstanding Volunteer. The more awards and honors you can muster, the more the colleges will think you are a winner (which of course you are).

Keep A Record Of All Of Your Accomplishments

You might think that you're too young for Alzheimer's disease, but you'd be surprised at how much you can forget in four years. In your senior year, you will need to recall exactly what you did since the first day of your freshman year. It might be easy to remember now, but in a few years it won't be.

To make sure that you don't forget, keep a record of everything you do. Include brief descriptions of your activities, especially if you made a special contribution to or were a leader of a special project, when you received a specific award or honor, what years you participated in activities, and an estimate of how many hours you spent on each activity. This list will help you immensely when you are completing your applications and will insure that you don't leave anything out.

Kiss Up To Teachers, Employers, And Advisors

Now is the time to set your pride aside, to dish out all the compliments you are capable of without gagging, and to hone your skills of flattery. Because you will need two or more evaluations from teachers, one from your counselor or principal, and possibly one from an employer or advisor, now is a great time to foster your relationships with these key people in your life. By the time you are ready to apply, your goal is to have them adore you as if you were their own child.

For current teachers, make sure that you participate actively in class. Yes, this means raising your hand and answering questions, volunteering to erase the board, and other such related sycophantic activity. Put your best effort into all of your work. Stay after or go early to ask questions. Try to volunteer to help your teachers with projects or try to give them extra help if they need it.

If it sounds like your goal is to become your teachers' pet, it is. You want to stand out from the other students in your class by developing a strong, personal relationship with your teachers. By doing this, your teachers will write the strongest evaluations possible. It will be evident that they feel that you are not only a good student but also an extraordinary person.

Also maintain your relationship with teachers after you have completed their courses. Drop by to chat when you have a free moment. Tell them what you enjoyed most about their class. Volunteer to help them in any way you can. Since you have already taken the course, perhaps you could help plan an activity for this year's course or give suggestions for a new way of presenting the material. Your object is to show your teachers that you are concerned and thoughtful enough to help even after you have nothing to gain from them (besides excellent evaluations).

To impress your employers, of course you should do your best at work. Be punctual, friendly, and the fastest burger flipper this side of the Mississippi. But also try to give extra effort by volunteering for additional responsibilities or working overtime when your employer needs the help. Get to know your employer beyond the employer-employee relationship so that he or she will be able to learn what kind of person you really are. Also, give feedback on your job and the company—what works, and if you feel comfortable enough, what doesn't. Even if you end up not asking your manager for an evaluation, your efforts may at least result in a raise.

Many colleges also want a report from a school counselor or advisor. If you are thinking to yourself, "Who in the world is that?" you are probably not alone. Many students do not take the time to really get to know their counselors until late in their high school careers. This can certainly be a disadvantage for these students when it comes time for their counselors to complete the school reports required by most colleges.

Make it a point to see your counselor or advisor as frequently as possible. Don't badger him or her, but drop by from time to time. Ask for advice on college planning. Consult with your counselor whenever you have academic or extracurricular questions. By seeking guidance and advice, you will emphasize your desire to pursue a higher education as well as insure that your counselor or advisor gets to know you well.

Avoid Appliphobia By Previewing Applications

Fear, anxiety, and nausea are perhaps the most common symptoms. Unfortunately, we're not talking about the flu. Rather, we are describing an acute case of "Appliphobia," or students' reactions to first seeing a college application. As you will soon discover, at first glance college applications are a maze of lists, questions, and blanks. They can be quite intimidating because they are about eight pages of questions that you must not only answer but must do so skillfully and thoughtfully.

That is why now is a perfect time for you to take a look at some applications so that you can overcome the effects of "Appliphobia" before you actually have to apply. Usually the earliest you can receive applications is during the late summer between your junior and senior years. However, you can always look at last year's applications to get an exciting sneak preview.

To receive an application, simply write a letter to the college requesting a copy. Addresses for admissions offices are listed in college guides found in most libraries. You can also ask your college counselors to see copies of some old applications.

Once you have an application or two, read through them. Not only will you find out more about the college application process, but you will also find out information about the colleges themselves. The applications are usually part of entire booklets packed with glossy photos of students so happy you wonder if they actually study, as well as information about the college ranging from its history to its academic focus to its extracurricular activities.

When you reach the actual application, you will find the basic components: the application form, essay, interview (sometimes), and evaluations. You will see that, yes, there is a lot of work ahead of you, but it is manageable, and you will be able to do it. By taking a look at the applications now, you will eliminate any surprises and be totally ready for the real thing. Who knows—you may even become excited at the prospect of packaging yourself to the colleges.

We hope this chapter has given you some ideas on how to prepare for your senior year. We highly recommend that you look over the other chapters of this book for more detailed information on the various areas of the application process.

Oh, and enjoy your few years of freedom from the stress of college admissions!

GROOM YOUR CHILD INTO HARVARD

• •

A PARENTS' GUIDE TO HELPING WITHOUT HURTING

In This Chapter

▲ A Galloping Overview Of The Admissions Process

▲ How To Pay For College Without Filing For Chapter 11

▲ 100% Freedom For Your Child: What? Why?

▲ Get An Early Start With Freshmen, Sophomores, & Juniors

The Difficult Role Of Being A Parent

As you probably have realized, things have changed since you were in school. And we're not just talking about hairstyles and fashion. In particular, competition has become astronomically fierce for entrance into the top schools.

Nowadays students spend a lot of time and money just preparing for college admissions. Many of our friends at Harvard attended special test preparation schools during the summer—some had even begun in *elementary school!* A few even hired so-called "educational consultants," who charged as much as *$100 an hour* to advise them on where to apply. How much all of this helped we do not know, but one thing was for certain: Their parents doled out hundreds and in many cases thousands of dollars.

It is safe to say that the competition your son or daughter will face will be extremely tough. Fortunately, you have two things working for you and your child: 1) Your child can use this book as a guide through every step of the admissions process (you knew we were going to say this, didn't you?); and 2) As a concerned parent, there are several things you can do to help. However, while your desire to help is sincere, we need to warn you up front that there will be times when you must combat your natural parental instinct to help your child because there are some things that your child needs to do solo. More will be said about this later, but first let's look at two things that you can do.

The first thing is to learn as much as you can about college admissions. Since by virtue of being a parent we know you are busy, we have included a brief summary of this process in the next section. Remember that what was true when you applied may no longer be so.

Another important thing you need to do is look into various sources of funding—hey, who do you think is going to end up paying for these four years of elite education? As you will see, there are many sources of funding you can take advantage of to help defray the costs of tuition. (We know this will make you smile.) But first let's take a look at the nuts and bolts of today's college admissions process.

A Galloping Overview Of The Admissions Process And How You Can Help

Unless your hobby is reading the latest literature from the College Board, you could probably use a refresher course on today's college admissions process. Although each area is examined in more detail in the various chapters of the book, the following is a quick overview of what is expected of your son or daughter and a few suggestions on what you should and should not do to help.

The Actual Application. This is the "stats" sheet for college admissions officers. It is a multi-page form for personal data such as test scores, academic honors, extracurricular activities, and work experience. With this information, the admissions officers get a quick summary of your child's achievements and can easily compare him or her to other students.

The main thing you can do is help your child pack the most impressive information within the very limited space of the application form. To do this, your child should emphasize the leadership roles that he or she has played in school and extracurricular activities. Admissions officers like to see that students are not just participating in activities but are also leading them. Your child should focus on any projects he or she has initiated and any special contributions he or she has made. Help your child to recall all of the things that he or she did during the last four years. Parents frequently remember significant events that their children overlook.

Even if your child has trouble keeping his or her room clean, he or she needs to keep the application clean. Since not much creative writing is required, what really counts is neatness. Because the application form is usually the last thing that gets done (often in the wee hours of the night), it is also where most of the carelessness occurs. As the final proofreader of the application, insure that every blank is filled and every appropriate box checked. Also make sure that there are no typos—misspelling the name of the school will certainly not improve your son's or daughter's chances—and if changes need to be made, make sure that they are done so that they are nearly undetectable. Tell your child to forget about putting X's through misspelled words and to use white-out or a new form instead. Make sure you get to see the final application form before it is put in the mail.

Essays. If you sometimes feel like you don't understand what goes on in the mind of your teenage son or daughter, here is an opportunity to find out. The essay, usually 500 words or less, is the admissions officers' window into the thoughts of your child. It allows admissions officers to form an image of the applicant beyond impersonal test scores and straightforward biographical information. Students often (although not always) focus their essays on themselves, their experiences, and their thoughts.

Since this is by far the most important part of the application, you should read Chapter 5 on writing the essay and even a few of the example essays in Chapter 7. As you will find, the college essay can be a very personal piece, and depending on how your child feels, he or she may not be comfortable sharing it with you. Respect his or her decision. It may sound strange that your son or daughter is willing to allow such a personal essay to be read by unknown college admissions officers and yet does not want mom or dad to see it, but it is certainly not uncommon. So don't take it personally if your son or daughter hesitates to show you his or her essay.

If, however, your son or daughter does not mind, then you should make yourself available for editing and proofreading the essay. One word of caution: Some parents get so overzealous in their desire to help that they end up nearly writing the essay themselves. This must be avoided at all costs. College admissions officers read literally thousands and thousands of essays, and they are able to easily spot the "mommy-daddies." These are essays clearly written in a style, with language, and on topics that betray the age and generation of the author. There is an instant rejection pile for these essays. So take care not to "edit" your child's essays to the point where your suggestions evolve into actually writing them.

That being said, try to be as objective as you can, putting aside for a moment your pride in your child, and give constructive criticism on the following points:

▶ Is the essay creative and interesting?

▶ Does it, within the first few sentences, draw you in and make you want to read more?

▶ Does the essay show a unique or outstanding attribute of the writer? This does not mean that the essay has to refer to the author overtly since the essay's style will also reflect on the character and sensibilities of the author.

▶ After finishing the essay, would you like to meet the writer? (Pretend that you haven't known him or her for the past 18 years.) Make sure that the essay does not make the writer appear too arrogant or meek or boastful.

▶ Does the essay make you think about the issues it raises? Are the issues raised applicable to your life?

▶ Are any parts of the essay unclear? Is there too much or too little detail?

▶ Do the paragraphs flow in a smooth and logical way?

▶ Is the essay true? Does it sound sincere?

▶ Is the image you form of the writer a positive one? (It may be very hard to be objective on this one!)

When you are finished reading, meet with your child to discuss your reactions. Try to make general comments or suggestions, and only use your red ink pen to make specific changes on technical errors such as grammar, punctuation, and spelling. Be honest, but try not to be overly critical. Praise the essay's strong aspects and offer positive solutions toward improving the weaknesses. No matter how busy you are, make yourself available to read your child's work as many times as necessary. Remember, each error you catch is one that the admissions officers won't.

Teacher And Others' Evaluations. The admissions officers already know that you think your child is the perfect candidate to attend their college. The evaluations provide the opportunity for teachers, employers, advisors, and others to verify this. These forms cover areas like your child's leadership ability, motivation, and ability to work with others. Without resorting to bribery (which we strongly disapprove of), there is not much you can do about them. You must fight your parental urge to intervene since it certainly won't help to badger your child's potential recommenders. They are the last people you want to annoy. Trust that your son or daughter has a pretty good idea of which teachers will write favorable evaluations. Do make sure that these evaluations get handed out to the evaluators early (two to three months before the application deadline) since it does take some time to compose a good recommendation letter.

Interviews. Interviews, required by many schools, can be downright frightening. Unlike the other components, they require interaction with real life admissions officers or alumni. Interview topics include everything from academic interests to hobbies to current events. They are also the time for students to ask questions of the colleges' representatives.

Fortunately, we walk your child through the interview process in Chapter 8 to ease his or her nerves. One of the best ways you can help prepare your child is to do a mock interview. At first, your son or daughter may be hesitant or embarrassed to do a mock interview with you as the interviewer, but encourage him or her to try it. In Chapter 8 you will find a list of commonly asked questions to which you can add a few of your own. The most important thing to remember is to give your child constructive feedback on his or her performance. Do not concentrate on weaknesses as much as strengths. Tell your child which questions he or she answered particularly well so that he or she will be confident during the real interview.

Also, never under any circumstances go with your child to see the interviewer. Some parents have the mistaken idea that it will help their child if they go in and explain what a good son or daughter they have and why he or she deserves to attend X university. Such attempts have a 100% chance of failing. Realize that the college interviewer wants to interview your child, not you. If you intervene, the interviewer will think your child is too dependent on you and not ready for the independence of college. Thus, unless you are planning to attend college together, you need to restrict yourself to helping your son or daughter prepare for—not do—the interview.

Grades And Coursework. This is not a radical idea, but naturally the harder the courses and the higher your child's grades the better. Again there is not much you can do but be supportive and encourage your son or daughter to take challenging courses. Avoid demanding that your child take the hardest courses offered all of the time, especially if they really are too difficult for him or her. (Most students take between two and four honors courses a year depending on what is offered and what they can handle.) Also avoid making your son or daughter do nothing else besides study. From friends' experiences, this usually results in triple bypass level arguments at best and total rebellion at worst. What seems to work best in instilling good study behavior is positive reinforcement through praise.

Test Scores. Your child will take what we call an alphabet soup of standardized tests some of which might include:

SAT I: Reasoning Test–Scholastic Assessment Test, with math and verbal sections.

ACT Assessment–Reasoning test with English, math, reading, and science sections. Usually students will take either the SAT I or the ACT.

SAT II Subject Tests–specific subject tests including English, math, foreign languages, social sciences, and sciences.

APs–Advanced Placement tests for attaining college credit during high school. Most students should take these tests after completing an Advanced Placement or honors course in the test subject.

PSAT–Preliminary Scholastic Assessment Test, given to juniors and some sophomores to prepare them for the real SAT and used as a basis for awarding National Merit Scholarships. Your child should take this test in the junior year and, if possible, earlier for practice.

There are many books available for helping your child prepare for the tests as well as numerous test preparation courses.

In general, if you can afford it and your child wants to go, you should allow him or her to take a test preparation class. The best time for students to take these courses is a couple of months before they plan to take the actual test. Most students who take the tests in the fall of their senior year usually take the test preparation courses during the summer between the 11th and 12th grades.

Don't expect miracles from any test preparation course although they have been known to happen occasionally, but do expect that by virtue of systematically studying for the exams and becoming familiar with their structure, your child will perform better.

We have also included strategies for self-study in Chapter 10.

That's it for the overview. Again, when you have some free time ("What's that?" you ask), refer to the specific chapters in this book for more details about what colleges expect. But, your main goal is to give your child positive encouragement and maybe to cut him or her a little slack when it comes to doing chores between October and January of his or her senior year.

How To Pay For College Without Filing For Chapter 11

After stressing you out with all that your child must do to be admitted to college, we are now going to try to help you relax a little by talking about how you can save some money. Each year the government and colleges award over $50 billion in financial aid. Even at schools like Harvard some two-thirds of all students receive some form of financial assistance. (Are you smiling yet?)

There are several forms of aid and some are definitely more desirable than others. At the top are outright grants and scholarships. This money has no strings attached, except that it must be used for tuition and does not ever have to be repaid. Next comes Federal Work-Study, which means that the government will help subsidize your child's wages for term-time work. This is helpful since it makes your child very attractive to employers on campus that would like to hire students to do research or office work but do not want to pay their full salary. Finally, various low-interest and deferred interest loans are often offered.

To tap into these funds, you and your child will need to fill out—you guessed it!—more forms. These include the colleges' financial aid forms which come with the applications, the Free Application for Federal Student Aid (FAFSA), the College Scholarship Service (CSS) Financial Aid PROFILE form, Federal income tax returns, CSS' Business/Farm Supplement, and CSS' Divorced/Separated Parent Statement. For details on each of these forms and whether you need to complete them, see Chapter 11 (no pun intended) and the instructions on the specific college application form. Colleges vary as to which forms they require.

Regardless of who completes the pile of paperwork, you will need to provide various information such as your annual income, savings, mortgages, loans, stock portfolios, etc. All of this information is kept strictly confidential and is used to determine if you meet the requirements for various federal, state, and college-sponsored grants and loans. Also, make sure that your child is aware of any special circumstances that your family has as a result of unemployment, job instability, a sick family member, other family members attending college, or a recent addition to the family. Colleges do take these factors into account, and they can have a huge impact on aid packages. Your child will receive a letter after being accepted at the college outlining the specific aid package offered.

If you are interested in all the ways your child can get outside scholarships from private businesses and organizations, you should also take a look at Chapter 11 where we have compiled a variety of strategies for finding and applying for scholarships.

However, don't forget that the most lucrative forms of scholarships are often the closest to you. For example, start with your employer. One student we know won a $20,000 scholarship from her father's company and $10,000 from her mother's union. Consider this one of the unwritten perks of your job. Regardless of who you work for, inquire about the availability of scholarships for children of employees. (If your company does not offer such scholarships, suggest to someone that they do.) Aside from your company, check with various professional and community organizations that you belong to such as your church, PTA, Lions Club, and Rotary Club.

100% Freedom For Your Child

Okay maybe you shouldn't give your child 100% freedom (possibly a frightening thought), but once your child is accepted to some colleges, you should give him or her as much freedom as your checkbook can handle in choosing where to attend. After all, it is your child–not you–who is going to be at the school for the next four years.

Obviously since you are probably the one who will foot a major part of the bill, you can express your preferences to your child; but for the most part, let him or her choose among the schools you can afford.

Both of my (Lisa Lee) parents are University of Southern California alumni, and if you are familiar with USC, you know that there is something so powerfully inherent in being a USC alumni that convinces you that your offspring, your offspring's offspring, and the next 17 generations of offspring must attend that college. Thus, when I earned a full tuition scholarship to USC and an additional scholarship that would have paid for my room and board plus given me a little extra for books, it was a very difficult offer to turn down.

Somehow, however, my mother and father combated their natural USC alumni instinct and allowed me to make my own decision about where to go. Now that they no longer have any tuition bills to pay, I think my parents finally agree with me that it was worth it for me to have no regrets about my decision to go to Harvard.

Be as supportive as possible about which school your child wants to attend, and emphasize that you are proud whatever his or her ultimate decision may be. After all, as we all know, it really does not matter which college your child goes to as much as what he or she makes of the experience.

Get An Early Start With Freshmen, Sophomores, And Juniors

As you may have guessed, Harvard students are not groomed overnight. Being the modest Harvard graduates that we are, we like to think that it takes a lifetime of training and self-discipline to reach the pinnacle of perfection. Truthfully, however, there is no regimen that you should have been prescribing for your child since birth. But there are a few things you can help your child do before his or her senior year in high school.

The earlier you and your child start thinking about the admissions process, the better. Chapter 12 is devoted especially to juniors, sophomores, and freshmen. To avoid repeating the same information, we have summarized a few points that apply specifically to parents.

Preparing in advance allows your child to select courses, get involved in activities, and cultivate relationships with teachers that will help him or her tremendously when it comes time to apply to college. Being knowledgeable about the admissions process yourself, you can encourage your child to make decisions that will help make him or her a stronger candidate.

The following are some guidelines for advising your child. Please do not force any of these suggestions on your child, especially if he or she is the kind of person who resists recommendations from mom or dad. But if possible, advise your child with these principles in mind.

Aim For A High GPA. Admissions officers see all of your child's academic records from the time he or she hits the 9th grade. If your child wants to attend a selective college, advise him or her that grades certainly count. Of course, it is not necessary that your child have a 4.0 grade point average, but the closer he or she can get to that, the better. The exception is when it comes to honors versus non-honors courses as explained below.

Don't punish your child for bad grades or bribe your child for good grades, but do encourage him or her to focus on studying. We know of some parents of our high school classmates who did not heed this advice and the results were disastrous. There was one student whose parents offered him a new car if he received straight "A's." The bribe worked for that semester and his parents were very happy. Unfortunately, it did not work when it came time for college admissions. The many rejections that he received from selective schools were due in no small part to the fact that he had started taking such classes as auto shop, wood shop, and speech to earn his high grades while his classmates were taking Advanced Placement English, Math, and Science. This example leads directly into our next point.

Don't Go For The Easy "A." In other words, encourage your child to take rigorous honors and Advanced Placement courses. It doesn't matter that he or she might be able to get a higher grade in an easier course. Almost all colleges recalculate grade point averages taking into account the difficulty of the courses. It is better for your child to get a "B" in an Advanced Placement or honors course than to get an "A" in a non-honors "gut" course. The first thing college admissions officers do when they open the transcript is note how many classes are honors or Advanced Placement.

Concentrate On Value Rather Than Volume. Encourage your child to lead, not follow. When it comes to extracurricular activities such as clubs, sports, and volunteer work, encourage him or her to make valuable contributions to the organizations. Admissions officers are more impressed by the quality of a student's participation in extracurricular activities–leadership positions held, honors won, programs started–than by the quantity of activities. Your child should work to attain as many leadership positions as possible and excel in whatever activities he or she chooses to join. Entering contests, publishing essays or poems, and starting organizations or clubs are also great ways for students to distinguish themselves from the thousands of other applicants to college.

Don't Groom A Bookworm. In addition to promoting strong study skills, allow your child to relax, have fun, and be a kid. Don't require that he or she study incessantly or take courses that are obviously over his or her head. After all, what good is it for your child to be accepted by Harvard if he or she is already burned out. Also, consider that academic achievement is not the sole basis for admission. Thousands of valedictorians are rejected from top schools each year. Colleges are looking for bright, but also well-rounded and interesting individuals.

Be Positive. Even the best students are not accepted by every school. Depending on each college's individual pool of applicants and needs, it may accept your child or may be looking for a student with slightly different, not necessarily better, skills. Do not push your child to attend one of the elite schools, and do not talk as if not getting accepted is equal to failure. Remember that even if your child does everything right he or she may, for reasons totally beyond his or her control, not get accepted.

A tragic but true story is of a family with two daughters who were accepted by Stanford. When the youngest child, a son, did not get in and had to "settle" for a state school, his parents did not hide their disappointment and frequently berated him as a failure. This boy eventually took his own life and from the note he left behind made it very clear that he could not live with the guilt of having let down his parents.

While this is an extreme example, you should be aware of how much emphasis you are placing, whether consciously or not, on your son or daughter getting accepted into a certain school. The truth of the matter is that college admissions is always a gamble to some degree and even the most qualified and deserving students are sometimes denied simply because the college does not have enough space in the freshman class.

Plus, as you already know, success in life is not dependent on where you go to school but on what you do there. Harvard and the other Ivies produce their share of losers. In the end the best rule is to support your child in his or her decision and to be proud of whatever the result.

DECIDE WHICH IVY GATE TO ENTER

In This Chapter

▲ The Waiting Game

▲ Parties & Other Important Criteria For Making Your Final Decision

▲ The Campus Visit: A Crash Course On College Life

▲ Stories From Real Life: How Awful Oxtail Soup Made Me Choose Harvard

▲ The Last Letter You Will Write To The Admissions Office

The Waiting Game

Mailing off your applications is a big relief. However, once it sinks in that the decision is now in *their* hands, the wait can cause more than a little apprehension. Unfortunately, there is not much you can do but wait it out. Each year admissions offices receive thousands and even tens of thousands of applications. Because each one needs to be evaluated individually, the whole process takes some time.

While there are variations among schools, most decisions should arrive at the beginning of April. Let us congratulate you in advance for all of the acceptances that you will receive.

If you want a hint, good news usually comes in thick envelopes, although this is not always the case since some schools send acceptances in business-sized envelopes—which some students don't even open since they are sure they are rejection letters. Inside, however, is a simple letter that reads something like, "Congratulations! You have been accepted. More information to follow."

The Quality Of Parties And Other Important Criteria For Making Your Final Decision

If the quality of parties is your highest priority in selecting a college, then you will have no problem deciding which school to attend. One student contacted the local beer suppliers surrounding the various colleges to which he was accepted. The college that purchased the most kegs of beer won his favor.

However, if you have more mundane criteria such as financial feasibility, academics, campus environment, class sizes, location, and extracurricular activities, then your decision becomes a bit more difficult.

Once you have your stack of acceptance letters, you will have the enviable task of choosing which school to attend. If you've been accepted at your first-choice school, congratulations on your accomplishment! Still, before you send in that acceptance card be sure to consider all of your options and never make a decision until you have your financial aid award letters.

Look back at the questions in Chapter 2 that you used to select where the apply. The same questions are still valid in deciding where to attend. In addition, now that money is a consideration, ask yourself the following questions to evaluate the economics of going to a certain college:

▶ Will you be able to afford to both attend school *and* eat? Before answering this, make sure you have read Chapter 11: *How To Win Free Cash For College.*

▶ What kind of financial aid package has the college offered? The financial aid letters will usually arrive after the acceptance letters. Be patient and wait to see what kind of offers you get.

▶ Is bargaining an option? Do you have an aid offer from another college that you can use for leverage?

▶ Putting aside the complex formulas that the colleges use, how much can your parents realistically contribute? How much of a burden will your education place on them?

▶ How long do you want your student loans to haunt you? How much do you think you can pay after you graduate? Don't be afraid to take loans, however, since your education is certainly a good investment.

Besides thinking about these questions, re-read the colleges' glossy brochures. Go to the library and look up your schools again in the college guidebooks. Also, speak with graduates from your high school who are currently attending the colleges, as well as alumni, teachers, counselors, family, and friends who might be able to provide you with some insight on the schools.

Some colleges will provide you with a contact number of a current student you can call to ask any burning questions. If not, call the admissions office and ask to be referred to someone who can answer your specific questions about the school. Don't be afraid to ask a question, no matter how trivial you think it may be.

It may sound nerdy, but make a list of the pros and cons of each school. Don't let the excitement of receiving the acceptance letter cause you to act too quickly. And never make a decision until you have heard from all of the schools.

Keep in mind that while choosing a college is one of the biggest decisions you'll have to make, there is still no absolutely right or absolutely wrong decision. All of the schools have their own strengths and weaknesses. Plus, no matter where you choose, you will most likely fall in love with it anyway.

The Campus Visit: A Crash Course On College Life

The best way to get the fullest picture of life at the colleges ranging from the quality (or lack of quality) of their cuisine to what it's really like to live in a 10 foot by 10 foot cage (i.e., the dorm) is to participate in the colleges' pre-frosh or visitation events.

These are usually one- or two-night stays offered by the colleges to accepted students. Often these include a stay in the dorm, meals at the cafeteria, and the opportunity to attend as many lectures as you can stay awake through. If you are adventuresome, you may even find a party or two.

During these pre-frosh events, you will usually also have the opportunity to meet your potential classmates; to speak with advisors, professors, and administrators; and to hear speeches about all of the wonderful reasons why you should attend the college. Most useful, however, is that you will stay with a current student in their dorm and be able to sample their lives for a few days.

If you cannot attend one of the college-sponsored pre-frosh events, you can still visit the college on your own. Walk around the campus, eat the food, sit in on a lecture, and visit the dorms. Don't be afraid to ask the students you encounter a few questions; they are usually helpful and will provide you with candid (sometimes too candid) answers.

Although you do not have to actually visit any schools to make a choice, we highly recommend that you do. Too many students have found out too late that the schools they selected only faintly resemble the glossy brochures, which quite understandably have a tendency to portray only the good sides.

Don't Wait For The Wait List

If you get Wait Listed instead of accepted, you may feel like you are living in a state of purgatory. It leaves your admissions status in limbo, suspended in between acceptance and denial. If not enough students who are accepted choose to attend the college, then students on the Wait List may be admitted. It is a way for colleges to insure that they have the right amount of students enrolled in the fall. Unfortunately, it is also a way to keep your life in flux by not knowing whether you will be admitted later.

If you are accepted at another school and know that you do not want to attend the school that has Wait Listed you, then you can remove yourself from the limbo state. Let the school know that you don't want to be considered for admission. However, if you would like to attend the school where you are Wait Listed, get used to the limbo state.

The good news is that you aren't completely powerless. There are a couple of ways you can demonstrate to the admissions officers that you would love to make the jump from the Wait List to the

How Awful Oxtail Soup Made Me Choose Harvard

Okay, I didn't really base my entire decision on oxtail soup, but it certainly played a role. Before I even applied to schools, I had already decided which college I wanted to attend. I am a native Californian and never fathomed living farther than an hour from the Pacific Ocean. Even though I had never seen the school, somewhere between birth and when I began to walk I just came to think of it as my dream school.

The school was very prestigious with a number of famous alumni. The beautiful glossy brochure from this college along with the flowery descriptions nearly sealed my decision that this was where I belonged. Besides, I only applied to Harvard on a whim, just to see if I could get accepted. I had no intention of living on the East Coast.

It was a couple weeks after I received my acceptance letters from both schools that I thought it might be a good idea to just consider Harvard as a possibility. I decided to visit both schools, starting with my dream school.

During pre-frosh weekend I discovered that my dream school had a few flaws. I was at a dinner for prospective students when they served incredibly awful oxtail soup. The fact that the oxtail soup (a personal favorite of mine) was so unsavory made me look at this school with a more critical eye. I soon discovered other things I didn't like: like the fact that it was way out in the country and I would need a car in order to reach civilization. I also realized that being a little father away from home and a change of scenery (and people) might not be such a bad idea.

When I visited Harvard I was totally impressed with the well laid out campus and beautiful brick buildings. I found the East Coast refreshing and exciting. The other students who I met were hardly the stuffy heirs and heiresses that I had imagined. In fact, they were pretty normal.

After visiting a few other campuses, going to classes, speaking with students, sleeping in the dorms, and of course eating the food, I came to realize that the college that I thought I would attend from the time I was an infant was not the place I wanted to spend the next four years. I ended up selecting Harvard and have never regretted the decision. And, by the way, Harvard's oxtail soup is quite delectable.

By: Gloria S. who loves more than the cuisine at Harvard.

accept list. The basic idea is to keep reminding them that they should admit you. Here's what you should do:

#1 Start out with the least confrontational approach by writing a letter. Write to the admissions officers to let them know that you are still interested in attending the school. Stress why you believe you should be accepted. Also, let them know about any great things you have done since you submitted your application, e.g. good grades earned or additional honors and awards won.

#2 Escalate to calling them. Verbalize your letter: Speak to an admissions officer about why you should be de-Wait Listed and what incredible feats you have accomplished. It doesn't hurt to drill this into their heads.

#3 Bring your teacher or advisor in on the act too. Ask a teacher or advisor to write or call on your behalf and present your case. It helps to have someone support you.

We hope that this helps toward de-Wait Listing you. Still, keep in mind that often colleges take very few students from their Wait Lists. If the college is one of your top choices, however, be proud that you tried your hardest regardless of the outcome.

The Deposit: To Pay Or Not To Pay

Some schools require a deposit to demonstrate that you are serious about attending. If you have decided that you will accept their offer of admission, by all means send them a check. However, if you are still waiting to hear from other schools and it is approaching the deadline, check with an admissions officer to see if the deposit is refundable (most of the time it is), then send it in. It's best to guarantee a sure thing than to risk not having your space reserved because you missed a critical deadline while waiting to hear from another school.

The Last Letter You Will Write To The Admissions Office

Once you've finished weighing all the factors, completing your research, and working out how to pay for your education, you can notify all the schools of your final decision. The only tip that we can offer about notifying the schools is that you make sure to do it before your selected college's deadline. This is one deadline you don't want to miss!

Once you have done this, all you have to do is wait to receive a collection of brochures, welcome letters, and, of course, bills from your new college. As for the college admissions process, you are finished! You've made it through one of the toughest, most stressful times in your life. Be proud of your accomplishment, enjoy the rest of your senior year, and get ready for the four best years to come! Congratulations!

A Special Request From Jim And Lisa

We would love to hear about where you will be going to college (and how our book may have helped get you there). Please send us a letter after you get accepted. You can send mail to:

Jim Good and Lisa Lee
c/o 101 Publishing
4546 B10 El Camino Real, Suite 281
Los Altos, California 94022

APPENDIX A:

COLLEGE ADMISSIONS RESOURCES & ADDRESSES

ACT Assessment Test–For a copy of *Preparing for the ACT Assessment* and an application for the ACT write: ACT, P.O. Box 414, Iowa City, IA 52243. Information: (319) 337-1270, Records: (319) 337-1313.

College Fairs–Schedule of fairs across the nation: National Association of College Admission Counselors, College Fair Desk, 1631 Prince Street, Alexandria, VA 22314-2818.

Common Application And Common Application On Disk–Accepted by over 200 participating colleges. Available from your school or: National Association of Secondary School Principals, 1904 Association Drive, Reston, VA 22091.

Free Application For Federal Student Aid (FAFSA)–Form you must complete to apply for federal financial aid. FAFSA Express Software– Software you can use to complete the FAFSA electronically. *Expected Family Contribution (EFC) Formulas*–Booklet that defines how your and your family's expected contribution toward your college education is calculated: Federal Student Aid Information Center, P.O. Box 84, Washington, DC 20044.

Funding For U.S. Study: A Guide For Foreign Nationals–Financial aid information for international students: International Education, 809 UN Plaza, New York, NY 10017-3580.

PROFILE From The College Scholarship Service (CSS)–About 900 colleges, universities, and scholarship programs accept or require this service in awarding aid. Available from your school or call CSS at: (800) 778-6888 or register online at http://www.collegeboard.org.

PSAT–Information: (609) 771-7070.

SAT I And SAT II–For descriptions, practice questions, and an application to register, get the College Entrance Examination Board's (CEEB) *Taking the SAT I* and *Taking Subject Tests*, available free from your school or by writing: The College Board ATP, Box 6200, Princeton, NJ 08541. Info: (609) 771-7600, Records: (800) 728-7267.

Test Of English As A Foreign Language (TOEFL)/Test Of Spoken English (TSE)–For TOEFL, TSE, and Test of Written English (TWE) information and registration materials write: TOEFL/TSE, P.O. Box 6154, Princeton, NJ 08541. Information: (609) 771-7100.

U.S. Department Of Education And Federal Student Aid Information Center–Federal Student Aid Information Center, P.O. Box 84, Washington, DC 20044-0084. (800) 4-FED-AID or (800) 433-3243. http://www.ed.gov. Useful publications from the Department of Education include: *The Student Guide: Financial Aid From the U.S. Department of Education*–Describes financial aid from the government and how to receive it. *Expected Family Contribution (EFC) Formulas*–Explains how the EFC formulas are calculated. *Direct Loans Repayment Book*–Provides information on how to repay a Direct Stafford Loan.

State Financial Aid–Call to find out which state agency to contact for state financial aid. (800) 4-FED-AID or (800) 433-3243. http://www.ed.gov.

APPENDIX B:

COLLEGE ADMISSIONS WEBSITES

Get Into Any College: Secrets Of Harvard Students
http://www.101online.com or http://www.webcom.com/101books/
The best free resource on college admissions and financial aid for
students, parents, and teachers. Features include: college admissions and financial aid articles, free e-mail newsletter, free articles
for high school newspapers and PTAs, resources for parents, college facts and fiction, and much more!

College Board http://www.collegeboard.org
Test information (SAT I, SAT II, PSAT, AP), registration, college
search, scholarship search, CSS PROFILE, online applications,
SAT question of the day, financial aid calculator.

Educational Testing Service http://www.ets.org
SAT, TOEFL information, test dates, practice questions.

Kaplan http://www.kaplan.com
Test information, preparation services.

Petersons http://www.petersons.com
Descriptions of colleges.

Princeton Review http://www.review.com
Test information, preparation services.

TOEFL Online http://www.toefl.org
Test dates, how to register, practice questions.

United States Department Of Education http://www.ed.gov
Student guide to federal financial aid.

United States Peace Corps http://www.peacecorps.gov
How to become a volunteer, where you can volunteer.

U.S. News Online Colleges And Career Center http://
www.usnews.com/usnews/edu/
Choose a college, rankings, guide for parents.

50 TOP COLLEGES (Alphabetical Listing)

Boston College http://infoeagle.bc.edu
Brandeis University http://www.brandeis.edu
Brown University http://www.brown.edu
California Institute of Technology http://www.caltech.edu
Carnegie Mellon University http://www.cmu.edu
Case Western Reserve University http://www.cwru.edu
College of William and Mary http://www.wm.edu
Columbia University http://www.columbia.edu
Cornell University http://www.cornell.edu
Dartmouth College http://www.dartmouth.edu
Duke University http://www.duke.edu
Emory University http://www.emory.edu
George Washington University http://gwis.circ.gwu.edu/index.html
Georgetown University http://www.georgetown.edu
Georgia Institute of Technology http://www.gatech.edu
Harvard University http://www.harvard.edu
Johns Hopkins University http://www.jhu.edu
Lehigh University http://www.lehigh.edu
Massachusetts Institute of Technology http://web.mit.edu/admissions/www/
New York University http://www.nyu.edu
Northwestern University http://www.nwu.edu
Princeton University http://www.princeton.edu
Rice University http://riceinfo.rice.edu
Stanford University http://www.stanford.edu
Syracuse University http://www.syr.edu
Texas A&M University, College Station http://www.tamu.edu
Tulane University http://www.tulane.edu
Tufts University http://www.tufts.edu
University of California, Berkeley http://www.berkeley.edu
University of California, Davis http://www.ucdavis.edu
University of California, Irvine http://www.uci.edu
University of California, Los Angeles http://www.ucla.edu
University of California, San Diego http://www.ucsd.edu
University of California, Santa Barbara http://www.ucsb.edu
University of Chicago http://www.uchicago.edu
University of Illinois, Urbana-Champaign http://www.uiuc.edu
University of Michigan, Ann Arbor http://www.umich.edu
University of North Carolina, Chapel Hill http://www.unc.edu
University of Notre Dame http://www.nd.edu
University of Pennsylvania http://www.upenn.edu
University of Rochester http://www.rochester.edu
University of Southern California http://www.usc.edu
University of Virginia http://www.virginia.edu
University of Washington http://www.washington.edu
University of Wisconsin, Madison http://www.wisc.edu
Vanderbilt University http://www.vanderbilt.edu
Wake Forest University http://www.wfu.edu
Washington University http://www.wustl.edu
Yale University http://www.yale.edu
Yeshiva University http://www.yu.edu

INDEX

FREE RESOURCES &
ORDERING INFORMATION

101Publishing, 4546 B10 El Camino Real, Suite 281, Los Altos, CA 94022
Order online: www.101online.com

Name:_____
Address:_____
City: _____ State:_____ Zip:_____
Telephone: (   ) _____ Email:_____
School: _____

YES! Please send me ___ copies of *Get Into Any College: Secrets Of Harvard Students* @16.95 each.

MAKES A GREAT GIFT! Please send___ copies @$16.95 each to:
To: (name) _____
Address: _____
City: _____ State:_____ Zip:_____

Sales tax: Please add 8.25% for books shipped to California addresses. Postage and handling: $4.00 for the first book and $2.00 for each additional book. International orders please add $7.00 for each copy. Please make checks or money orders payable to: 101 Publishing.

___**ACE YOUR ESSAYS!** Please send me more information about Jim and Lisa's one-on-one essay-writing counseling service.

___**FREE!** Please sign me up for your **FREE EMAIL NEWSLETTER.**

___**FREE FOR TEACHERS & COUNSELORS!** Please send me ___ copies of your FREE *Get Into Any College: Secrets Of Harvard Students* financial aid and college admissions newsletter.

___**FREE ARTICLES FOR NEWSPAPERS & NEWSLETTERS!** Please send me FREE articles I can print in my school newspaper or newsletter, PTA newsletter, or any other publication.

___**MEET JIM & LISA!** Please send me more information about arranging a speaking engagement or seminar with Jim Good and Lisa Lee.

Visit our web site
www.101online.com
The best FREE resource on college admissions and financial aid for students, parents, and teachers

MORE ABOUT THE AUTHORS

Together Jim Good and Lisa Lee earned acceptances to every college to which they applied: all of the Ivy League schools plus other prestigious universities including Stanford, Berkeley, Duke, and Rice. Jim and Lisa recently graduated Magna Cum Laude from Harvard with degrees in history and sociology, respectively.

The authors also earned over $55,000 in merit-based scholarships to help pay for the cost of their Harvard educations. The awards ranged from a National Merit scholarship to a local Lions Club scholarship as well as many in between.

Before getting into Harvard, Jim attended a small public high school in a rural part of Oahu. Between eating banana flavored shaved ice and basking in the sun, he was president of the Student Council and captain of the Speech Team. He was also active in the Mock Trial team and played tennis. Jim was the first student from his high school to be accepted at Harvard.

Lisa attended Whitney, a nationally ranked public high school in Los Angeles. She was the editor of her school newspaper and yearbook. She founded a public service club to promote literacy and worked part-time having the awesome responsibility of shelving books at the local library. Even in a highly competitive environment where everyone dreamed of going to an Ivy League college, Lisa was able to stand out from the rest.

Jim and Lisa spent over three years researching and writing this book which makes extensive use of the experiences, secrets, and strategies of dozens of other students at top colleges.

Both Jim and Lisa are firm believers that writing a winning application is an "art" and one which can be learned. After spending many years researching and cataloging the ways in which other students have been accepted at the most selective colleges, they believe that they have written the most comprehensive book on the subject. The lessons in these pages will help *any* student who wants to get into *any* college.

Jim and Lisa currently call Northern California home.